Mommy's Little Girl

Susie Bright
on
Sex,
Motherhood,
Porn,
&
Cherry Pie

PRAISE FOR *MOMMY'S LITTLE GIRL*

"Anyone interested in sex, family, and relationships will want this book."

-Anne Semans, *The Good Vibrations Guide to Sex*

"Bright is one of America's most vocal sex-positive advocates, offering her sexual liberation message in advice columns, personal appearances and books (Susie Bright's Sexual Reality, etc.). This collection of 22 sketches written during the first 12 years of her daughter's life covers a variety of topics: her daughter's problems at school when she reveals her mom works as a sexpert, how nudists look when they age, the ubiquitous use of Viagra, her feelings about a friend's suicide and even a recipe for cherry pie."

- *Publishers Weekly*

"I laughed out loud, got weepy and felt generally inspired to live a fuller, more satisfying sex life."

-Abby Ehmann, *Eros-Guide.com*

"Susie Bright is the Molly Ivins of Sex. She's honest, intelligent, funny, and such a good writer! I enjoyed every one of these wide-ranging essays. If you don't want to think about sex, she's not for you, but she always avoids being preachy or simplistic. I found her descriptions of her interactions with her daughter touching and believable... it's so hard to give your kids the tools they need to stand up against the uniform terror people seem to feel around sex even now. A good read!"

-Harold S. Henry, *Amazon.com*

"Reading Susie Bright's latest book *Mommy's Little Girl* is like sitting down to a cozy cup of tea and a long chat with a loving, brilliant, witty friend. I sent this book to my own mother, a former librarian, who informed me that this book comes under the category of "guilty pleasures." Read, enjoy, and learn, from one of America's most beloved advocates of erotic freedom!"

-Linda Rowland Jones, *Amazon.com*

"An enlightening, frequently engrossing, often laugh-out-loud-funny read. In one essay, "Dirty Bookstore Docent," she tells a friend, "Going to these places [old school porn shops] is like visiting a museum -- you need a history lesson, a decoder ring, and an experienced docent if you want to have a clue as to what's really going on." And that's what Bright is, in *Mommy's Little Girl:* a dirty docent to the paradoxical world of the multifaceted sexual being. "We're walking, we're walking," you imagine her intoning, as she gestures grandly in the direction of the topics taken up in these essays: words of wisdom about sex spoken to her daughter; some foreshadowing of the Viagra craze; octogenarian nudists; a day on the set of a porn film; (sex) life on book tour."

-Polly Pagenhart, *LiteraryMama.com*

"Susie Bright is the genuine article; she proves the point that the muse screws, that all creativity is inevitably sexual, and that the juiciest people write the most delectable books."

-Erica Jong, author of *Fear of Flying*

Mommy's Little Girl: Susie Bright on Sex, Motherhood, Porn, & Cherry Pie

Copyright © 2008, 2003 by Susie Bright

ISBN 0-9708815-7-6

Published in the United States by *Bright Stuff,* P.O Box 8377, Santa Cruz, California 95061.

Book design, cover photography, and production: Terese Jungle. Author photo of "mommy and baby" by Jon Bailiff.

Printed in the United States of America
Second Edition
ISBN:987-0-9708815-7-6

This book is dedicated—like any devoted mother—
to cherished little girls everywhere.

ACKNOWLEDGMENT

THIS IS A COLLECTION of stories I've written over the first dozen years of my daughter's life.

When I originally pitched a version of this book to the publishing world, many editors were dubious; they told me I couldn't be a sex goddess and a mom at the same time.

Because of such inspirational doubts, let me first give thanks to all those conservatives who unintentionally spurred me on.

This collection starts out with stories that are primarily about my daughter Aretha in her younger years—and yes, she has vetted them before publication. She was the most ruthless editor of all. She is now a teenager. It must have taken a lot of fortitude to endure my preoccupation with every word that came out of her mouth.

As I worked on this collection of stories and essays, I thought most keenly about what I'd learned about sex and family over the past decade. I shared my essays with my partner Jon Bailiff, my father Bill Bright, my managers Jo-Lynne Worley and Joanie Shoemaker, and my writing friends Linda Rosewood-Hooper and Jill Wolfson. Jon deserves more credit for the cherry pie than he's ever going to get.

Some of the stories in this book started out as essays for editors Laura Miller at *Salon*, and Jim Petersen at *Playboy*, among others. I've learned a great deal from these editors, and I appreciate all their encouragement and good humor.

Finally, I have to thank all the readers who wrote to me and inspired me with so many questions and arguments—you are the best. I hope this book leads to a lifelong conversation.

Susie Bright

CONTENTS

Mommy's Little Girl

CHERRY PIE

mommy's little girl

MY MOMMY'S JOB

I WAS SLIDING ON MY BUTT around the kitchen floor, trying to force my sick cat to swallow a giant blue pill, while my eight-year-old daughter, Aretha, stood over us, watching with complete disdain.

"So, I need to know, what is your job, Mom?"

I got the capsule in the back of the cat's gullet and clamped his muzzle shut. There was something I didn't like about Aretha's tone

"What do you mean, 'What is your job?' "I imitated her prissy tone." You know perfectly well what I do. I write. In fact, we just spent fifteen minutes in the car together while I complained about my latest contract"

Aretha's eyes narrowed and her hands went to her hips. It was so unnerving to stare up at this haughty queen that I stumbled getting to my feet.

"No, Mom," she said, in a voice so loaded with sarcasm that by all rights, I should have evaporated on the spot "I need to know what it is that you do exactly when you 'write' "

I had scraped my palms during the pill tussle, and Little Miss Superior had not even begun to get the cat food out as I had requested five minutes before this inquisition began. I decided to let her have it.

"Look, stop treating me like crap and tell me what's going on with you, because the last thing I need after I've been doing my job all day is for you to talk to me like I'm not worth two cents." This time I was the one with a tone of voice; I was loud and mean. She shrank and turned around to leave.

My bite was worse than the cat's. "Don't you dare walk away from me. That's even worse." She still had her back to me, but I could tell she was crying. I softened. "Is this something about school; are you supposed to write about my job for your homework?"

She nodded. "It's for Ms. Stein's class," she wept. Ms. Stein is her writing teacher.

"Aretha, we talk all the time about my writing—you were just teasing me today that I haven't written a book all about *your* life yet! Do you really not understand what I do? Or are you embarrassed by what I do?" The second I said the word *embarrassed,* something curled inside my chest like a crushed leaf.

Her head sank down. "The last thing you said," she whispered, as if to spare my feelings by not repeating it. "I didn't tell you this... it happened a long time ago. (That could mean anything from yesterday to three weeks ago.)

"I was standing in the cafeteria line, and this boy who I don't even know poked me in the back and said, 'I know what your mom does. She writes about S-E-X!' "She started crying harder." And he was singing it like it was a dirty song and I wanted to slap him so hard that his head would fly off because it's none of his business, and it was so *humiliating,* and now Ms. Stein is making us write a paper about what our parents do for a living and—"

"You don't want to say that I write about sex because everyone will get hysterical—"

"And they all think sex is disgusting and I don't want them to hate you, and I hate this paper because I don't want to answer any personal questions!"

All of a sudden, I felt as if I needed a fainting couch. "Can we go lie down and talk about this?" I asked.

In truth, I had been waiting for my daughter to come to me with this problem since I first became pregnant I remember how people would ask me—even before they inquired about christening names or the sex of the baby—"Aren't you worried about what your child will think of what you do?" They would look at me gravely, as if a great sorrow were about to unfold.

I had one acquaintance, a sex therapist, who called me up twice to warn me: "If someone like you has a daughter, she will hate you. And there's nothing you can do about it. I brought home a box of tampons when my kid was twelve, to talk about her period, and she screamed at me that I was a slut."

I didn't know what to say to all the "well-wishers" who warned me how ill fated my motherhood would be. Something like, "Wow, thanks for the heads-up. I'll schedule an abortion right away"?

Instead, my defense was to consider my own childhood. I got bullied for so many things: thick glasses, pathetic social skills, orthopedic shoes, homemade clothes, and, most of all, for being a kid who didn't have two parents at home. My mother divorced in the sixties, and at the time grown-ups remarked upon it in hushed tones, as if she were gravely ill. One high school English teacher I had announced in front of our entire class that she couldn't help it if I was "from a broken home." I thought that was ridiculous, but when I told my mother, it broke her heart.

I know what it's like to survive being a "weirdo," and I concluded that you can't build your life around a fantasy of conformity. Those kids who had all the right labels going for them weren't happy campers either—as I found out later, when they became my friends. I was proud of my mom and how we lived, even if I didn't like my awful shoes and glasses.

Yet now, Aretha was breaking my heart with her story. If only I were a nurse! A children's librarian, an Avon lady! I wanted to protect her from all the bullies, no matter how much that might concede to their ignorance. "You don't have to write about me at all, honey," I said, "You could write about your dad's job, or your godmother's, or anybody's you want."

"I don't want to write about them. I want to write about you," she said. Her stubbornness surprised me.

"Well, I know your teacher feels fine about my books; she would never make fun of you."

"She's not the problem." Aretha sighed, and of course she was right.

"Look, you asked me the other day what 'ethics' is," I said, "and it was practically impossible to explain. But this—this is a perfect example. If you choose to, you never have to say 'sex' in your paper, and you can talk about all the other things I do when I write. But if you don't say it, you might feel like you have to keep this awful secret that makes you feel ugly inside. Sometimes it's worth it, in the long run, just to say, 'My mom writes about sex, so grow up and get over it!' "

Aretha frowned. "No, as soon as I say 'sex,' they will all start laughing and then they might ask me questions like, 'What *kind* of sex' or, 'Is it man-woman sex?'— and I don't want to talk about it!"

16

"Oh, they make me sick," I said, "Every single one of them is going to have sex with someone someday, and then they'll wish they hadn't spent so much time obsessing about how disgusting it's supposed to be"

Aretha didn't have much interest in the future karma of her tormentors. "So you don't care if I don't say you write about sex?"

"No, I don't care at all. I just want you to pay attention to your feelings, and see if you feel okay later about making a secret like this. I don't want you to feel like you can't be yourself and be proud of your family."

"Not all secrets are bad," she protested. "Like when you have a present for me and it's a secret or when we want to surprise someone and it's a secret."

"Yeah, those are fun secrets—you're right this is different. It's the kind of secret where you feel like you have to hide something about yourself because other people won't like you. Sometimes people just aren't worth it"

Aretha handed me a Kleenex box, because this last bit of advice made me start crying again. "I honestly don't know what you should do," I sobbed. "I just know one thing: this is a really hard assignment and I can guarantee you that a lot of other kids are freaking out right now about what they're supposed to write."

She looked at me like I was daft. "Nobody else's mom writes about sex!"

"No, that's not what I mean...I mean, there are kids in your class whose parents don't have any kind of 'job.' What are they supposed to say? We're getting food stamps right now, but the welfare office is cutting us off in two weeks'? Or what about the kid whose folks are growing pot or the kid whose mom is a lesbian insemination doctor? What if your dad was a toilet plumber?"

"A toilet plumber?" Aretha howled and fell off the bed, screaming. "Omigod, a stinky toilet plumber man!"

Finally, I had come up with an alternative worse than being a sex writer. "You know, a toilet plumber makes a lot of money," I said. "If I were a toilet plumber, we'd probably have a new car and a swimming pool. And they work on something that everybody *has* to have, but they're embarrassed sometimes to say what they do because everyone laughs at them and thinks it's gross, just like you."

Aretha became quiet and looked as if she had taken this to heart. Finally, a sense of righteousness was upon me, and I knew what I wanted her to do: "Look, I don't care what you say about me, but I want you to promise me that you won't laugh at a single other student's paper, because you know now how hard it is to write something like this." I crooked out my little finger to her so that we could make a pinky-swear vow.

She curled her pinky around mine and squeezed. "I promise," she said, but her eyes were far away. "A swimming pool, for real, Mom?" she said. "I wish you *were* a toilet plumber! "

FIRST-GRADE VALUES

IN 1996, MY DAUGHTER ARETHA learned how to read and write. It was a miracle because I didn't understand how it happened and it seemed to appear all at once.

When Aretha graduated first grade, I sat with the other amazed parents in Room 7 at Longview Elementary, listening to the children chant, "And now I'm six, and I'm clever as clever, and I think I'll be six forever 'n' ever."

Just how clever were they?

Ordinarily, if my daughter called me a nasty name in public I'd have had a swift punishment to deliver. But when she got angry with me over breakfast dishes and wrote "Mommy is a pig" in purple felt pen on her self-decorated bedroom walls, I was close to tears of joy. My baby is expressing herself! —and her spelling is already better than that of many of her adult relatives. I had told Aretha she could draw on her walls, and now she filled them like pages of a diary. She was the living embodiment of the First Amendment.

Aretha learned more in her sixth year than the strange rules of the English language—she got inculcated with the even stranger rules of American values. The things my daughter brought home her first-grade year on the subjects of sex, race, and religion made me want to wash out the entire mouth of our crazy world with the strongest soap I could find.

Take the last week of school, for instance I picked her up on a Monday afternoon, with tears and snot running down her face "What happened?" I said, a phrase I repeated like a broken doll all schoolyear long.

"We were playing the Power Game," Aretha sobbed—which, as she described it further, sounded like a sadistic cross between Jonestown and "Simon Says," although it's one of those ephemeral games the kids make up at recess. "One person has 'the power,' " Aretha explained, and they get to make all the other players do whatever they say."

The goal of the other players is to "Take it" with as much stoicism as possible—not to crack. Aretha was in post-tournament pieces.

"Who plays this horrible game?" I asked, and Aretha paused her crying for a moment. "It's the *Power* Game," she said, as if that explained everything—and then, as if it were an afterthought—"No Mexicans can play, though."

I had to watch it when we had these conversations in the car because I was wearing out my brakes. "It's a *Power* Game and no *Mexicans* can play?!" I plowed into a curb.

Our family lives in a beach town that's part university, part hippies, a lot of farmland, and a sprinkling of Silicon Valley interests. As in much of the state, the majority of the population is Latino, but an overwhelmingly white political and business elite runs the show. Her school is probably a quarter "American," and she can actually include herself as part of the majority; her birth father's family are native Californians and Mexicans.

When Aretha and I got home, we looked at a map of the world. I showed her where Mexico is, and reminded her that she is half Mexican-Indian herself. I gave her a thumbnail history of Mexican and California Indian history, which I'm afraid she got a bit mixed up with the Disney *Pocahontas* script—but I'll take my antibigotry lessons where I can find them.

I told her that in fact, none of the kids in her class are "Mexican"—that's just something idiots who don't know better say. I knew all the students in her class, and except for one Yugoslav, all were born in the United States. A handful lived with parents who were primarily Spanish speakers, but they were not exclusively Mexican, either. Her homeroom was bilingual. At the same time, the white and white-passing kids—*las gueras,* like my daughter—were picking up all the social cues that they were the real players in life

The hardest part about these talks with my daughter was when she asked me the hard questions—like why the Spanish treated Indians like slaves and children, and why the Anglos went even further, exterminating tribes like vermin.

"Why did they treat them like that; how could they be so cruel?" she asked.

"Yeah, well, why are you playing the Power Game?" I shot back. "You all don't even have any money involved."

Another afternoon, another showdown.... "I'm going to clean up after the boys today so that we can get ice cream," Aretha said when I dropped her off at school in the morning. "Miss Rogers says if we don't clean up after our snack, then we won't get ice cream—and the boys never do it, so I'm going to clean up theirs, too."

"I'll give you a double dip of *anything* you like if you promise me you'll never clean up after a boy again," I said, in the first spontaneous bribe I ever made to her. "You start now and it never stops." She was impressed and made the bargain with me.

I took her and her girlfriend Katie for double-dip chocolate cones after their last class. They sat quietly in the car until

Aretha spoke out of nowhere—"Mommy, all the girls at Longview giggle really hard when someone says 'sex.'"

"Do *not* say that word!" Katie squealed, in perfect emphasis.

"Katie," I said, risking who knows what repercussions with her parents, "if it weren't for sex, you wouldn't be here, so maybe you should lighten up." I turned off my broken air conditioning so the car actually became hotter, but quiet. "Some girls get taught by their parents to be embarrassed about sex. But you don't have to be silly about sex; you know better."

"But sex is for when you get married," Katie insisted, and this prompted Aretha to jump in with some special school yard gossip on the subject. "Lorena is going to kill herself if she doesn't get to many Rafael!"

I gathered that this was a direct quote from Lorena. "Does Rafael know about it?" I asked.

Aretha and Katie burst out laughing—of course not. The boys are clueless, playing kickball while the three princesses-in-training sit at a lunch table and formulate their wedding plans.

Aretha didn't yet have all these ideas strung in a row. She was in awe of wearing a wedding dress, but her favorite T-shirt was emblazoned with the slogan "GIRLS RULE." She had a mind to influence the masses, and the Room 7 recess crowd could thank our family for making the word *clitoris* as commonly understood as *penis* on the playground. During recess, those kids talked as much about sex as any crew of construction workers. But sometimes Aretha had her own entirely independent opinions, separate from me or her school, and those were the most provocative of all.

Another time, during the First Grade of a Million Questions, she asked, "How come Sandy and Jared don't take their clothes off when we go in the pond?"

"Because their family believes in a god that thinks the naked human body is shameful, and we don't," I answered.

"But do you believe in God, Mommy?"

Another one of those impossible questions! I never knew that one day I would feel shy answering a little girl. "I believe that there are big things I don't understand," I said, wanting to be tender. "I believe in being humble but I don't believe in some god in the sky telling people how to live."

She looked sideways at me, uncharacteristically coy. "Don't you want to ask me; don't you want to know who I believe in?"

I was a little fidgety. We were sitting on my bed underneath my gigantic five-foot hanging plastic rosary. A bronze Krishna figurine stood on the dresser next to my classic Barbie, and a book of Greek myths lay on the floor in a pile of dirty laundry.

"Okay, Aretha, do you believe in 'God'—what do you think?"

"I believe in *all* of them," she whispered, lifting her arms around her in a swirl. "And I pray to them, too." Her eyes shined, and I wondered what kind of prayers she'd write on those walls, next to the drawings of a pig.

CHECKMATE

WHEN SHE WAS EIGHT, my daughter received her first lesson in chess from her godmother. Honey Lee. She has now played a total of three games with other people. (She's also been playing against herself—or some imaginary loser, I don't know who but those games seem to end rather quickly.)

I don't know a rook from a rooster, but I am captivated by watching her play. She's very emotional and surprisingly rowdy. She whistles loudly while her opponent is contemplating the next move, and she had one big cry when her dad, Jon, "stole" her knight, as she put it. Instead of saying "Check," she sings out, "POP goes the weasel!"

I picked up the beginner's instruction book (Chess Basics, highly recommended) to see if this is part of the chess vocabulary.

"Oh yes," said Jon, "that's what Fischer said to Spassky in Reykjavik." I really didn't know whether to believe his story because I did find a story in the book's gamesmanship chapter about two adult champions, Petrosian and Korchnoi, who, in a 1977 tournament, kicked at each other under the table until a below-the-waist partition had to be built to separate them.

I am riveted by Aretha's competitive spirit and her desire to win and gloat. Early in her very first game with Honey Lee, she warned, "When I'm done with you, your life won't be worth a penny." I was never encouraged to play like this when I was a child. I fantasized about knocking balls across the field to the amazement of my schoolmates, or beating a grown-up in a simple card game, but I was afraid of being immodest or competitive in public.

The one contest of any significance I won was a spelling bee. Although, I was initially disqualified because the judge, our principal, made a mistake with the three-letter word it's... as in, 'It's a beautiful day.' "I spelled it with the appropriate apostrophe, and he triumphantly rebuked me, "No, that's wrong. The correct answer is I-T-no apostrophe-S."

I would never have contradicted his mistake because that would be "talking back"—arrogant, and a whole lot of trouble. Later, some teacher who obviously didn't give a shit about such an outcome, pulled me into the head office and introduced me to the principal again, who grimly announced, "There has been an error. You have won the spelling bee" He handed me a gray piece of paper with the Riverside County Schools letterhead on top. I gathered there would be no publicity.

My fear of competition and my desire to "make nice" weren't just academic liabilities. They were also the first aspects of my sexuality I confronted when I began to have sex with other people If my lover touched me in a way that was displeasing hurt—or just didn't rock my boat—I would rather have died than said anything about it I instantly grasped the technique of faking orgasm, because it was as familiar as faking satisfaction about anything else when courtesy demanded that I not speak up. I also wouldn't show what I wanted with my hands. That too, would have drawn too much attention to myself.

My salvation was that I read a lot, which introduced me to the notion that I would be happier if I pleased myself sexually. Betty Dodson said so! I traded in one set of authority figures for another. Most persuasively, I had a couple of blunt lovers who shattered my ideas of what could and couldn't be said aloud between friends.

"The way you kiss—it's terrible," my first girlfriend told me. She was French, so I thought she must know what she was talking about. She gave me kissing lessons and explained the way she wanted me to caress her mouth. I was grateful after the initial bum of embarrassment. Another of my early boyfriends flat out asked me, "Why don't you come with me? I don't like it as much if you don't. You masturbate, don't you? Show me!"

Well now, there he had me ... if I were to please him, then I would have to have an orgasm. It wasn't a matter of being self-centered.

Many years later, when I started writing prolifically about sex, my readers imagined me to be an erotic Catwoman—on the prowl, taking what I wanted with style and endless nerve. The truth is I'm more like a mouse that encountered some radical manifestos and was inspired through sheer outrage and hunger to roar, accidentally overcoming my original character and training.

Will my daughter be a tiger because of feisty genes, or has my encouragement to "use your power" taken effect? I've deliberately given her opportunities to do unladylike things. I've tolerated and defended her aggressiveness in speech and in movement. I never wrestled on the floor when I was a girl, but she loves it. When she asks for boxing gloves, I deliver. I never talked back, but Aretha thinks nothing of arguing if she believes she's in the right. That kind of assertiveness training is the hardest to endure of all.

What sexual advice have I given her? I've left it very open as to what sex is—that it's any two (or more—I'm so careful) people touching each other all over with their hands or mouths or genitals. She really doesn't know yet that when most people say "sex," they mean only penis-vagina intercourse.

I've given her a few direct words about bodily fluids and STDs, but I don't harp on it. That's what she's going to hear from everyone else—how adult sex is so dirty, disease-ridden, and dangerous that it's amazing that anyone would want to go through puberty and attempt it. I tell her that sex is supposed to feel good, really good; if it doesn't, you should stop what you're doing. I tell her, "Don't worry about hurting the other person's feelings if you don't like the way it feels. It's your body, after all. They would want the same consideration from you."

She gives me a puzzled look, as if to say, "Duh, Mom! Why would I do anything that made me feel bad?" I have a hard time explaining why I've done all the things I've done that made me feel bad. I'm just a mixed-up kid, on the threshold of the second change of life—who knows what kind of balls I'll have to come up with next?

"Baby," I say, "I hope you have this rowdy confidence as long as you live"—because honestly, whose life is worth a penny without it?

THE BIRTHING DAY PARTY

ARETHA CELEBRATED HER TENTH BIRTHDAY for almost a month. She traveled to Disneyland, performed her first handstand in the pool, braided her hair into a hundred little strands with butterfly clips, and held a Monopoly marathon with all her friends. She went out of town to visit another round of admiring relatives and friends, leaving strict instructions for me not to read any new novels before she did.

Sometime after settling a six-girl argument over how to auction the Boardwalk property, and before inspecting our blistered feet from Tomorrowland, I had a fleeting moment of introspection: I'd been a mom for ten years as well. Trying to comprehend my place in the past decade of my daughter's life is the Maternal Time Machine. It seems like yesterday when I was in the throes of the proudest sex act of all time—childbirth—yet I can hardly remember any of my daughter's early moments without prompting from the family photo albums. When did I blink? How did this baby suddenly become a mini Amazon?

At her birthday party, as I tucked the girls in for the finale sleepover, I asked them if they had any "birth stories," what their mothers had told them about the time they were born.

Trina, the guest with the quickest repartee, snickered. "My mom says it was a "non-event.' "She posed with her fingertips curled in the air, to imitate her mother's emphasis with air quotes.

Her description made me cringe, but Trina didn't catch my reaction, pleased as she is in her own wit. I turned to the other girls, realizing that they all looked a little low on information.

"My mom had a *ci-so*—, *cee-saw*—" Maya was struggling.

"Cesarean?" I asked.

"Yeah!" she said, relieved not to have to finish the pronunciation.

Carrie, the smallest, recognized something. "My mom did that, too, with me and my brother." She stipulated, "And he took longer than me." She rolled her eyes as if this behavior had never stopped.

"I had an emergency cesarean with Aretha, too," I said, "after trying a vaginal delivery for many hours."

As soon as I said the word *vaginal*—in fact, the second I hit the first syllable, "vag," all the pillow tussling and sheet tugging stopped. For the first time in an all-day party, there was absolute quiet. I felt twelve little eyeballs on me, the girls' collective breath in midgulp. I realized that the nonchalance I'd had in using this word and the rarity of its mention in most households had just hit critical combustion.

Like all the other ten-year-olds I've met, these kids are no strangers to first-class potty talk. They break down in hysterics singing songs about farts; they die over the boy in sixth grade who had to be sent home because he caught his pee-pee in his zipper. They whisper all the nastiest words from the latest R-rated movies—their parents won't let them see those, yet the lexicon is commonplace playground knowledge. Still, even the gnarliest R-rated action flicks rarely refer to female genitalia or pleasure, except maybe as something that smells bad. These girls, like all American women, would have to be influenced by something other than popular culture in order to hear a word like vagina, let alone clitoris, vulva, or labia.

Before this particular moment, none of them had said the phrase "vaginal delivery," even though it's something that most people go through, so to speak. For them, even "cesarean" is difficult to say—it remains mumbled and jumbled, not because of its phonetics, but because of what it refers to: the taboo world of women's bodies.

A couple of the girls in my daughter's classroom have already begun their periods; the others will probably begin in the next three years. They have encyclopedic information about subjects as diverse as Japanese anime, the entire Gap kids clothing line, raising pit bull puppies, and naming the coolest surf breaks in town. But their idea about how babies get "made" is right out of a 1950s marriage manual.

Sure, they know that a "sperm meets an egg" and they know the general area between the woman's legs where the baby "comes out." But they don't have any sense, let alone detail, of the changes and capacities their female bodies go through during puberty, pregnancy, childbirth, or menopause They don't know that they are amazing female children whose bodies are about to experience tremendous changes in the next decade.

Some of my friends would say, "Well, why should they? They're only ten, what do you expect? Let kids be kids!"

This sentiment seems to imply that knowing your body parts and basic physiology ruins one's childlike imagination and innocence But these are the same kids who had to write a report about their favorite animal last year, including its breeding patterns. They performed plant propagation experiments in science lab; and in the grade before that, they had to make a 3D collage of the entire insides of the human body—the heart, lungs, brains, muscles. The collage included *everything* except the genitals, because that particular piece of ignorance is considered essential to grade-school biology.

More pointedly, both girls and boys know all the proper and slang names for boys' genitals—*dick* and *balls* are stock giggle items throughout the school yard. The girls know that boys urinate through their penis—and also when they're older, are able to have "have sex" with the same piece of equipment.

But what do girls "have sex" with? Most girls don't know. They know that boys "get off* with these penises of theirs; but they're not sure whether they have something that would make them feel the same way.

Spare me the nineteenth-century illusions about childhood's precious blankness. These girls are smart and inquisitive. They are experts at bathroom humor. But they are also deliberately kept ignorant of their intrinsic female anatomy—to the point of not even knowing the names of anything below the waist

Instead, their curiosity and sexual tension gloms onto peripheral topics: what the boys are doing what the *boys* think of them. They agonize over their first bra, but they have no idea what breasts are all about, other than something the boys find sexy. They think that breast size (and a matching set of lingerie) is what makes you womanly, rather than breast sensitivity and arousal, or the capacity of their breasts to nourish a new life.

I know my daughter is unusual in her education, but hardly alone. Like a lot of moms who were influenced by the seventies' feminist healthcare revolution, I looked forward to raising a daughter who would know all about her body, from her elbow to her vulva. I imagined a new generation of women who would carry a sense of confidence in the natural functions of their bodies—whether that was eating dreaming or appreciating sensual touch.

I want girls to know—like *every* little boy does—that there is a part of their genitals that is simply for sensual pleasure, as well as a part that facilitates childbearing. The clitoris is a remarkable part of a girl's body, and it doesn't have anything to do with babies (other than perhaps providing some ancillary motivation to conceive one). I don't want to see any more young women turn thirty years old before they understand what a female orgasm is.

This kind of parent-to-daughter education doesn't involve unbearable privacy invasions or long textbook discussions with medical manuals. It's as natural a conversation as anything your kid may bring up, like celebrating a birthday. Children love to hear about how special their actual birth date was.

When my daughter's friends fell into a hush over the little bits and pieces of information they'd heard about their entries into the world, I made a leap of faith: I asked them if they'd like to see the pictures of Aretha's birth.

Aretha caught my eye and gave me her traditional warning. "Oh, Mom!" I realized she was warning me not to get too mushy, not to embarrass her with my sentimentality. But she also sensed the intense curiosity among her playmates, and she hurried me into the other room to retrieve her birth album. This revelation was dearly raising her friends' interest and her social cachet.

I rummaged through the bookshelves and felt a little sweaty— what I was about to show might very well get reported to five other moms—and then what? Would they be outraged? Would some little miss never be able to come over to our house again? Or might they be incredibly relieved? "Send your kids over to Susie's house; she makes sex seem so wholesome!"

I felt the same wallop that invigorated me when I was a teenager, reading _Our Bodies, Ourselves_ for the first time: Dammit, girls have a right to know this! I don't want to shelter girls from their own self-interest.

I brought out my album of childbirth snapshots, which opens with me pacing around the hospital floor, looking like a spectacled Humpty Dumpty. I thought everyone would laugh at how round I was, but instead they all cooed, "Oh, you look so young!" Ouch! Thanks for the honesty, angels.

They marveled that I was able to be in labor and simultaneously get my toenails painted by a friend. I explained that birthing could be a tedious process sometimes. I described labor: Contractions are what make the baby move down through the womb, and a little tiny passageway called the "os" grows from the size of a dot—I squeezed my fingertips to illustrate—to the size of the baby's head. "That's *incredible!*" Maya gasped, *"How bad does it hurt?"*

Aretha interrupted me to point out the bowl of red Jell-O next to my hospital bed, which she considers the culinary highlight of the whole event. We went off on a tangent about why the doctors don't want you to eat anything if there's a chance of surgery.

"You know, my mother never told me anything about childbirth," I said, "except that she screamed her head off until they put her to sleep with a shot and she blacked out.... That always scared me."

Maya nodded her head briskly, as if this story sounded *de rigueur.*

"But when I got older," I told her, "I started helping my girlfriends with their births. And I realized that it doesn't have to be like that. Even when there's pain, if you know what your body is doing you know that every contraction is moving your baby out into the world. The intense part ebbs and flows like a big wave."

I saw Carrie's gaze drift when I said this, and I could imagine her on her dad's longboard, lifting herself onto one of the peaks.

The next photo was the big climax. The girls all squished in to see the first photographic peek of Aretha emerging—her little legs, toes, and butt coming out first. "She's so tiny!" they cried. Aretha squirmed, unable to explain why she towered over most of her fifth-grade peers.

"Yes, and look at her tiny, perfect, little face," I said, pointing to my own favorite photo. "This is the moment when the midwife placed Aretha's head next to mine, and I touched her, my finger on her cheek for the very first time... my heart just burst."

"Mom, *pu-leeze!*" Aretha tugged on the edge of the album. She wanted to stop the gooey talk.

"Oh, give me a break," I said, peeling her grasp from the book. Ten-year-olds are such dictators.

Trina, who had uncharacteristically not said a word for the past several photographs, squinted at me, making a face

"There is no way your birth was a 'non-event,' " I said, pulling her into my lap. "You are so precious, and you are all so lucky to be girls, because you can be born *and* give birth; you get to see *both* sides of the beginning of life"

"But I can't remember seeing anything!" Aretha cried, as if she had been given a terrible seat at the theater of life.

"That's what's so amazing, honey," I said, "because you get to have a second chance."

I looked over for the photo album and saw that Maya was snoring on top of it. It was practically midnight, and none of us were going to be able to see anything straight pretty soon.

"I *can* remember seeing something," Trina said, burrowing under her cover. And with that confession, every one of them fell asleep.

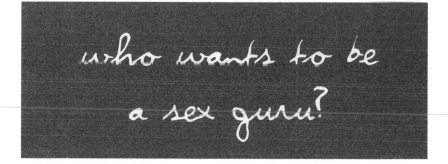

HOW TO RUIN ANY WOMAN'S SEX LIFE IN THIRTY DAYS OR LESS

I GOT A PHONE CALL FROM *COSMO* magazine, asking me to contribute a tip for their upcoming feature, "How to Improve Your Sex Life in Thirty Days." The title of such a venture gave me some doubts. I hated the whole notion of tightening up your libido the way you would a set of abs.

After a fruitless conversation, I hung up the phone, depressed by their orgasm-indifferent attitude toward women's sexual pleasure. They think improving your sex life means tricking your date, rather than making a significant erotic impression on yourself. To comfort my wounded soul, I logged on to my freelance writer chat group, where there are many popular forums for writers' complaints.

"I always get asked the same tired questions by these women's magazines," I wrote in the "Pissed Off" topic. "I wish someone would ask me how to *ruin* their sex life in thirty days."

One of my colleagues, Mary Elizabeth, quickly posted her response: "Who needs thirty days?" That made me laugh aloud: How right she is!

Destroying your sex life is a snap, compared to enjoying it. I decided to devise a list of a dozen libido-killing strategies that any seeker of the sex-free lifestyle should be able to accomplish well before a month is up.

Mommy's Little Girl

(1) *Don't admit your sexual desire.*

Single gals, go ahead and play the dating game all you want—the important thing is never to admit that you have a sexual interest at stake. *Shop* for the perfect marriage, but make sure that all your efforts are for romance or God's will. Follow the "Cock-teaser Manual" page by page, and rest assured that none of it will make you hot, horny, or sweaty. If you make the right match in the proper state of sexual ignorance, you may elude the clutches of lust altogether.

Some of you bad girls who have been around the block may have dabbled in sexual pleasure in the past. Now it's time to straighten up and fly right. You're a wife and mother now—do you want people to think you're some disgusting slut? If you don't have a headache by now, start sniffing glue.

(2) Stay *indoors.*

This is one of those subtle but surefire strategies to shut off unwanted outbursts of sensuality. You don't *want* to feel the sun on your face. Remember. It causes cancer. Flowers will activate your allergies. Fresh air and exercise might wake your clitoris out of its coma. (If you're the type to stand in the middle of a storm singing "It's Raining Men," there's really nothing we can do for you.)

(3) *Throw your diary in the trash.*

Self-reflection is a one-way ticket to erotic speculation. One moment, you're innocently recording your dreams—and the next thing you know, your pen is scribbling an illicit fantasy. There you are, acting sexy without even taking your clothes off! It's time to stop "expressing yourself," and begin expressing a little self-restraint.

(4) *Blame it on the kids.*

This is a tip for the parents among you. If you haven't ceded your connubial bed to your children by now, you are under the mistaken impression that there should be some standard of privacy in your home. You don't want your kids to think that you actually *do* the *deed,* do you? Don't make them *sick.* If the stork was good enough for Grandma and Grandpa, it's good enough for you.

(5) *Remember: Your body is disgusting.*

Take off all your clothes. Look in the mirror while standing directly under a fluorescent light. Notice any flaws? Of course you do; make note of them out loud and also in writing. Now, begin a new habit of mentioning those same flaws to your family, friends, and acquaintances *every single day.* Extra points for imposing your self-deprecating remarks on total strangers.

6) *Go on every crazy diet you ever heard of.*

While you surveyed your figure in your mirror, I'm sure you noticed one indisputable fact: you are grossly overweight. I don't care where you tip the scales; the fact is, you're a fat pig. Get cracking and start that cabbage soup diet. There's enough liquid protein enema solution for everyone. If you've only flirted with anorexia and bulimia before, it's time to get serious. Did you know self-starvers and bingers don't *ever* have orgasms?

(7) *Get religion.*

Embrace a faith that demands that sexual desire be sacrificed to achieve a higher goal. It doesn't matter whether the aim is enlightenment, a first-class seat at the pearly gates, or a special appearance on your gum's fund-raising campaign.

Tired of old-fashioned churches? No problem—plenty of "New Age" disciplines are just as repressive as their "Old Age" counterparts. Find one of those cults where no one gets laid except for the old fart at the top.

(8) *Don't play with yourself.*

'Nuff said.

(9) *Buy something.*

Did you know that *every* erotic urge can be repressed by a rigorous round of retail therapy? Don't hesitate to buy things that are *advertised* as something that will make you feel sexy. These unsatisfying purchases will simply titillate you into buying more—and will never, ever result in your having actual sex. Go out there and shake your moneymaker!

(10) *Covet what you can't have.*

Assume an envious position. The more you pout, the less chance you have of noticing any opportunity that does come your way.

(11) *Give yourself a label and stick with it.*

Stop fighting stereotypes and start advertising yours. Don't budge an inch from the personal-ad description you wrote five years ago. When you're certain you know exactly what box everyone else fits into, you're less likely ever to get out of your own.

(12) *Shut up.*

Talking about sex honestly with other people makes most of us uncomfortable. Get a clue, and stop trying to have that conversation!

Talking about sex leads to *thinking* about sex—and before you know it, you're back to step one: *thinking* you might like to *have* some someday! Cut it out. Once you've finished reading this map to sexual destruction, for goodness' sake, don't mention it to anyone.

THE REAL MAN'S GUIDE
TO LOUSY SEX

"WHAT ABOUT MEN?" you ask. "Aren't they also entitled to break the bonds of fleshly rapture?" Well, of course they are! Yet, taking into account how important gender stereotypes are in ruining *anyone's* sex life, we must approach the male animal with an entirely different strategy from the one we use for the fairer sex.

First of all, no real man can brag that he wants to rid himself of sexual desire. The mature woman can freely boast that she doesn't care if she never has sex again, with almost complete social acceptance but the manly man must at least *appear* to be effortlessly and inexhaustibly horny.

Many men are already ambivalent about sexual intimacy, or feel burned out from erotic heartbreak. But to maintain a sufficient masculine image, they *must* seem to be perpetually on the make. As a result of this ugly form of schizophrenia, we have legions of men who despise women, but who will chase skirts into eternity. Here we have the makings of a superb erotic breakdown.

Some of you may be saying "But, Susie, I'm such a cream puff—when I'm between a woman's thighs, savoring her soft body in my arms, I turn into a big love bunny."

Well, my little pet, we must put you on a special regimen. Our goal is to shrink those pesky emotions like a bunch of hemorrhoids. In no time at all you'll find that you can't get laid to save your life.

Ready to hit bottom? Here we go.

(1) *Faking it isn't just far girls anymore.*

It's not your come shot you should fake, it's the so-called emotional connection that so many pansies insist is simultaneous with orgasm. Say "no" to that soft spot melting in the center of your chest. Disconnect as quickly as possible. Don't let the odd second or two of vulnerability bewilder you! Get it in and get it off. You'll be thinking about carving the next notch in your belt before you can say Casa-fucking-nova.

(2) *Accelerate your sexual dysfunction by pretending that you want to score ALL the time.*

Variety may be the spice of life, but mass quantities are where the real bargains—and bragging rights—become yours forever! The more people you touch *only* with your penis, the harder it will be to arouse the little fellow—and what an elite company you'll be in. Live for conquest, and soon you'll be living alone!

(3) *Obsess about you inadequate dick size.*

Measure it; fret over it daily. Bite your lips bloody while you scrutinize those compelling penis-enlargement ads. Sure, they *say* that the operation is dangerous and disfiguring—but that's just what *all* the big-cock guys say to keep the franchise to themselves! Whether you elect surgery or not, the key is dedicating yourself to relentless feelings of inadequacy. Clearly, your penis is not as big as it should be. And as everyone knows, it's virtually the only thing women are concerned about. You can hardly open the personal-ad section of a newspaper without seeing another long list of chicks advertising their demands: "Single female seeks penniless, carefree dude with gigantic member."

(4) *When in public, avoid eye contact.*

This is the geek master's shortcut to never having to worry about unwanted casual connections.

(5) *If you do find yourself in a "conversation" with a potential partner, make sure it's a one-way dialog.*

You do the talking—*all* the talking. If she seems about to interrupt you, it's time to cut her off. Take out your cell phone for a nice flourish—accentuate the fact that you don't have the time to listen. Obviously you won't have time to eat her pussy, either.

(6) *Set an impossible standard for your dream girl; women will be too bamboozled by their own insecurities to question it.*

Why should you cast your balls before swine? You know that the only person who could truly appreciate you is last year's Miss September centerfold, and she's probably an old hag by now.

(7) *Get married.*

When I ask real men for suggestions on how best to ruin a guy's sex life, "get married" is the first thing that pops out of their mouths. Not a bad idea! But it only works if you make sure that your bride was never interested in sex from the first day you met. You want to marry someone so naive that she has no grip on what turns her on in the first place. That way, you can blame *your* inhibitions on *her*. She'll be the one who put your sex life on ice, and you'll never have to take the rap. This one stroke alone will also help you to achieve the next step:

(8) *Hold onto that double standard.*

Remember: When choosing a serious partner, avoid those slutty girls who enjoy orgasms and bodily fluids. Find yourself a girl whose "virtue" is beyond compare—literally. Obviously, a woman who likes sex as much as you do will never be good enough to be the mother of your children. Save those bad girls for times when you need a guilty little secret.

(9) *Listen to your peers.*

When well-meaning buddies tell you to conform, to avoid sexual and emotional risk, to doubt your lovers, or to expect the worst in love, buy them another drink. Engrave their warnings on your heart. (You may have so-called "friends" who are actually encouraging you to open your heart—they're obviously losers whom you want to avoid).

(10) *He who has the most toys wins the Viagra prescription.*

Nothing makes sex more irrelevant than a healthy appetite for material goods. Here you've been worrying about love, when all you needed was a new SUV! A faster hard drive and a precision audio system could make you happy—really. Who needs an ugly erection when you have a beautiful high-yield portfolio?

(11) *Stay in touch with your masculine side, 24/7.*

Big boys don't cry, so don't go all soft on me on a bad day. If you start getting mushy again about your "feelings," we're going to have to remind you that if you're going to *feel,* you're going to get *hurt,* and we'll have none of that!

(12) *Graduate to granite.*

You're all set! By the time you've finished this amazing program, I promise you, you'll be hard as rock, inside and out. Some of you may indeed be fortunate enough to have cut yourself off from most of humanity. What a relief.

As for those of you who can't cut it—you big silly love bunnies with a rocket in your pants—give me a ring and leave me your phone number. You obviously need the personal attention that only a trained expert can lavish—excuse me, I mean lash—on you.

THE BUZZ OF THE CENTURY

THE LAST TIME I WAS IN TEXAS, a young man stood in a line at a bookstore to meet me, and when we finally greeted each other, he asked me if I would say a prayer for him. I'm no minister—merely a traveling sex guru—but where human sexuality is concerned, I'm accustomed to people pleading for supernatural help.

"Brother, I'm happy to light a candle, but tell me what it's for!" I said to him.

"Sister, I'm going on trial tomorrow morning here in Texas for selling a vibrator," he told me, "and I could face a lot of time."

God have mercy on us. Texas, along with Georgia and Alabama, has laws on the books that criminalize the sale of sex toys, much to many of their citizens' amazement. Alabama allows for penalties of "up to $20,000 and up to one year in jail or hard labor," for selling any "device useful primarily for the stimulation of human genital organs."

Clearly, certain politicians have made a sport out of persecuting bedroom behavior they neither understand nor appreciate. Now, thanks to what may be the most talked-about history book of the year, we have the ultimate vibrator politics expose, a book by Rachel P. Maines, called *The Technology of Orgasm: Hysteria, the Vibrator, and Women's Sexual Satisfaction.*

I wonder if Senator Tom Butler, the sponsor of the restrictive Alabama sex-toy code, knows that vibrators were invented in the late 1800s as a "time-saving device" for physicians to treat the condition of hysteria among their women patients. Yes, even in the South, doctors were practicing this very medicine!

What did the doctors mean by "hysteria"? They weren't talking about anything a quick slap to the cheeks could remedy. No, as Maines reveals, the diagnosis of "hysteria," from the times of ancient Hippocratic medicine, has been described as the upsetting symptoms that women exhibit "on account of a lack of sufficient sexual intercourse, a deficiency of sexual gratification, or both." Many doctors considered the two conditions to be exactly the same thing.

Whether the ill women were fainting gasping not sleeping or throwing fits, they were often diagnosed with a sort of "womb fury" that the experts were sure was a sexual and reproductive malaise. Spinsters, widows, and overripe virgins were especially suspect.

Maines has documented the history of Western medicine's interpretation of women's sexuality, and it is dismal indeed. A woman's climax was thought of as a "hysterical paroxysm;" sometimes to be avoided, and at other times to be purged through various kinds of stimulation.

This is where the handy vibrators came in—doctors would electrify their patients into post-hysterical relief. The medical sages were so ignorant of the role of the women's clitorises, and so certain that women must necessarily find completion in coitus, that even when they gave these "massages" to their female clients, it appears most of them had no awareness that, in effect, they were having sexual experiences with their patients!

As Maines says, "The evidence suggests that doctors called disease paradigms as they saw them." Nowadays, we would simply call such "hysteria" pure horniness, with a little ladylike frustration thrown in.

At the turn of the last century, doctors were embracing new technology. Vibrator treatments were the perfect method to keep patients coming in for a condition that never went away, yet was happily relieved by this wondrous quick fix. Hysteria treatments revealed the commercial appendix to the Hippocratic Oath: Time is money, honey!" Doctors were eager to try the new machine that cut treatment time for such patients from the better part of an hour to a few explosive minutes.

How did Maines discover the buried secrets of vibrator history? She certainly didn't go looking for it. In the early seventies she was a student in classics, with an emphasis on ancient science and technology. She began to do serious research in the history of textiles, particularly the home knitting and crocheting world dominated by women.

She accepted a position at Clarkson University in New York and continued studying women's magazines, which specialized in the sewing crafts. To her amusement, along with the rhetoric of knit-one, purl-two, she found vibrator advertisements in every journal she read. As she explains in her preface, "My reaction to their turgid prose was to assume that I had a dirty mind."

Clarkson University thought Rachel was a naughty girl, too. When she first published her controversial 1989 article on the history of the vibrator, they fired her, fearing that alumni would stop giving money if they imagined their funds were going to such salacious research.

But Maines had a *brilliant* dirty mind, and she could not ignore genuine historical phenomena. The old advertisements for vibrators were everywhere she looked, from *Women's Home Companion* to the Sears-Roebuck catalog. As she began to make inquiries about the origin of vibrator manufacture, she found the devices among the *top five* personal electric appliances sold for home use—right up there with the toaster, tea kettle, sewing machine, and fan—and preceding the vacuum cleaner by a good ten years!

The heyday of these vibrator ads was between the early 1900s and 1930s, during which brands such as White Cross Electric promised, "Swedish movement right in your own home! Just a few minutes' use of the wonderful vibrator and the red blood tingles through your veins ... the same treatment you would have to pay at least $2 each in a physician's office!"

Yes, the buzz was out—for the cost of few visits to the doctor, you could have your own vibrator for years, and use it as often as you pleased.

As you can tell by the advertisements' euphemisms, they did not speak of sex or orgasm directly. In pictures showing customers using the product, the models placed the devices on their lower backs or on the tops of their heads. This bizarre innuendo continues to this very day with many vibrator manufacturers, who still put labels on their products saying things like, "Do not use on unexplained calf pain," even though no one in the know has any intention of using a vibrator that far below the thighs.

Vibrator advertisements only began to fade from the world of women's magazines and family catalogs with the advent of celluloid pornography, the popular stag film. As vibrators began to make erotic appearances in various blue movies, it became disingenuous for advertisers to make claims for the wholesome vigor of their products. The "pornification" of vibrators was thus spearheaded by the technology of motion pictures; it was this new prurient attitude toward "electric massage" that has left its legacy on Alabama and Texas legislators today.

It wasn't until the 1970s—after a century of deceit—that feminist sex educators cheered the genuine benefits of electromassagers out loud: the fact that vibrators produce an exciting sensation when placed on, or near, the glans of the clitoris.

Electric vibrators give most women an instant hard-on—and can bring them, if they so desire, to the orgasmic threshold. Many women who have never experienced orgasm before get a literal jump-start from their first vibrator. The consequences are, of course, delicious; a woman in touch with her orgasm is no longer hysterical.

Feminists also put clit power on the map and made it known that it was entirely unrealistic to expect most women to come from straight fucking—i.e., vaginal penetration with no external clit stimulation. Some men still question this idea, but perhaps it's because the process is not usually explained to them in terms of their own orgasm. There are women, a small but genuine minority, who can be excited to climax through pressure against their vaginal walls. That is, after all, the only way to massage the "back room" of the clitoral body, since only the glans, the little bud, is visible on the outside A woman's glans is just like the glans (head) of a man's penis; it is the most sensitive part of her genitals.

There are also *men* who can orgasm simply through someone licking their balls, or from prostate stimulation. But it's no secret that *most* men would like some primary attention to the head and shaft of their penises, if you expect them to climax anytime before next Sunday.

Many anthropologists have asked, as Maines has: Why is it that coitus, the act required for procreation, does not give the most efficient means of stimulation to the woman as well as the man? No one has the answer—as yet—but at least we're finally asking the right question.

Nowadays, we enjoy the attitude that sex is more enjoyable when both lovers are happy, and that female orgasm is a healthy part of a woman's physical experience.

Some vibrator virgins may be saying, "Well, you hardly need a mechanical device to stroke a woman's pussy!" And of course they are right. Tongues and hands, not to mention plain ol' bumping and grinding have brought pleasure to millions.

What has been intoxicating to women about the vibrator (and the same goes for a nice strong stream of water, too, as Maines explains in her bathing section) is that the intense, quick pressure of vibration accelerates the first rush of arousal in a way that most women don't experience as frequently as men do.

Women often feel as if they are "slow pokes" compared to men in terms of getting hot—with the exception of certain hormone surges, or the heightened occasions of falling in love, or breaking a taboo. Men, on the other hand, have often envied women for their ability, once they *are* aroused, to keep going and going and going and going... Timing is everything and men and women sometimes pass each other right by as they attempt an ecstatic connection. Vibration is one clever way to make a bridge.

While some male readers might consider Maines to be male-bashing in this regard, (or at least ego-bruising), it's dear that women must also account for their part in the double-standard charade. Are women bold enough to come out of the orgasm closet? I'd say that when it comes to lovemaking, we have paid a cruel price to fake it.

INTERN PHOBIA

I'M SOMEONE WHO NEEDS a lot of help. I often wish there were a half-dozen little clones to get all my domestic and professional duties accomplished. Whenever I can afford to, I've hired a house cleaner or contracted a baby-sitter to come on a regular night. In my home office, I regularly recruit part-time secretaries on whom I lavish uncorporate wages, copies of X-rated videotapes, and true tales of the horrors of the publishing industry that leave them gasping. The sex business pales by comparison.

In my years as an employer, I have learned this, by tearful experience: *Never* hire an intern. Never let anyone work for free, or even for pennies. I don't know what advice the White House would give you, but my lesson on interns is that if you expect to get one bloody thing done in your office, the last thing you need is someone who worships you. Interns will eat you alive. My message, as echoed by the Clinton legacy, is that you get what you pay for.

I encountered my first intern when I was pregnant in 1990, looking for an apartment in my fifth month, and feeling a little anxious that I was going to end up with a shopping cart and a sleeping bag instead of a carefully tended nest.

Many of my fans had read my articles about expecting my first child, and I received all sorts of congratulations and speculative horoscopes in the mail. The most interesting letter I received was a handwritten note, with a Polaroid attached, from a long-haired, red-headed, cross-dressing man. He offered his immaculate service as a laundry maid. He promised it all, from fluff 'n' fold to French cuffs. The photograph showed him hard at work

in a frilly maid's outfit leaning over a hot ironing board. Wow!
I had three loads waiting to go!

I called a friend of mine in the dominatrix trade that afternoon
to ask if she could school me in any etiquette I needed to know
in accepting this service.

"Freeze right there," she said. "I threw that exact same bastard
out of my apartment last week." He had pitched the identical
deal to her as well! "He thinks every time he turns on the spin
cycle, he gets to have a hard spanking. You'll never get your
wash done!" Load for load, Mr. Petticoats expected that laundry
day was going to be our "special" time together.

Undaunted by one bad apple, I experimented with other volunteers. I emphasized our common goal of sexual revolution, and
I stressed that every revolution has its fair share of paperwork
and heavy lifting. On one occasion, I took on a team of seven
male volunteers to host a women's salon, only to find that one of
them had disappeared two hours into our project. "What happened?" I asked his comrades.

"He realized he wasn't getting laid." But he hadn't said a word
about it during our interview! I was so naïve.

Actually, female interns are scarier. If I had just given
Mr. Disappearing Act a quick blow job, he probably would
have sweated for hours at my bidding. Maybe I really would
have lower dry-cleaning bills if I would just break out the cat o'
nine tails once in a while.

But when it comes to young women, they want more than a
tickle. Sex is almost beside the point. It's the erotic conquest
that captivates them, and God help you if you're not ready to
deep-throat their entire romantic fantasy.

I once had a secretary who gave up a lucrative assignment to work for me, her "role model." I was embarrassed that I couldn't afford her regular rates, but she insisted the pay cut was nothing. She refused money for gas, or postage, or the bagels that she brought to my office. For my birthday, she gave me a little silver bell that she said could ring "whenever you need me."

A few days later, she called me at home and told me, sobbing that she was quitting and that she'd never felt so disrespected in all her life. Why? She told me many reasons, none of which seemed compelling. Apparently I had dropped a soiled Kleenex in the front seat of her car. I couldn't shake the feeling that I had scorned her unwittingly—I hadn't used that little bell the way I was supposed to.

I was wrecked. I felt like a boor and a bad employer. I stared at her in-box in despair. I don't know how long I sat in my dark basement office before the doorbell rang and I heard my roommate at the top of the stairs, giggling: "Uh, it's *another* belated birthday present for you."

I went to the door to find a plump little pigeon of a girl dressed in a red bow and a G-string with big brown puppy eyes, and a note attached to her corsage. She whispered, "Maria sent me... I'm yours to do with whatever you wish."

I looked into those big brown puppy dog eyes and knew that my wishes were completely irrelevant. It was another damned "intern." They won't let up until they've sucked you dry.

"I really can't fuck you right now—do you have car fare home?" I pressed money and a sweater into her hands. She looked distraught, but I knew by now that you can't end these things fast enough.

BOYS WHO WANT BURGERS

Advertisement One:

A man contemplates a sexy woman who appears before him—
she seems to crave his attention. He recognizes that she would
jump in the sack with him at the slightest encouragement Yet,
in the comer of his eye, he sees a brand-name beer waiting for
his pleasure at an adjacent table The beer wins his attention;
the foxy lady doesn't stand a chance.

Advertisement Two:

A young man repeatedly chooses a big juicy taco over the invitation to score with willing and available girls.

Advertisement Three:

Another young man is being observed in a laboratory environment. He is offered a delicious cheeseburger or a gorgeous, sexually available babe.

Overcome with his good luck, the man gasps, "You mean I get
to choose between a girl and a burger?" After a moment of suspense, he picks the girl.

One of the lab observers turns to the other, and remarks, "What
an anomaly! No one's ever done that before."

Is this a joke? Sort of. But this punch line is cracking wise today because, like the best jokes, it has a grain of truth to it.

Welcome to the new breed of healthy young men who rate
sex way beneath their other appetites. They find girls a pain, a

disappointment. They would rather be satisfied with a brew and bit of beef than an erotic tide of passion.

Advertising agencies are capitalizing on the younger generation's penchant for irony—yet there's a kernel of authentic confession in each of these promotions. Lots of guys today have sexually retreated, or soured on the mating game altogether. You don't have to search out Miller Time or Taco Bell to find them.

Traditionally—say, since the dawn of sexual stereotypes-men have been the ones who were horny all the time, supposedly thinking with the little head instead of the big one—fools for a pair of long legs, soft tits, and a welcoming smile It was women who were appointed to say no, who always put the brakes on lust in favor of their virtue or respectable climb to success. A woman who made an ass of herself over a sexual affair wasn't unheard of—but she learned her lesson quickly.

When feminists and sex researchers started talking about women's sexuality in the late 1960s, it became dear that one reason women didn't feel connected to their sexual self-interest was that so many of them had never had sexual satisfaction to begin with. Finally, many liberated women spoke up, admitting that they'd never had an orgasm, and that they didn't know where to begin.

Sex is the one area men are supposed to excel in, by default. Their penises are so obviously 'there"; their practice of masturbation practically demands itself. They get an added helping of testosterone, and the same amount of encouragement to be virile that girls get to be chaste.

So when we see men today who are ambivalent about sexual companionship, is it because they are losing their orgasmic pleasure? Or do they lack desire altogether? I've come to the conclusion that the answer to both these questions is yes. I've heard the confessions of many men, of all ages, that they are not finding sex to be as compelling or satisfying as it "used to be" Some say that relief from their desire is a thing to envy. Sure, there are still plenty of horny men who will bark like a dog to get laid. But the big news is that so many men, and so many young men in particular, are as ambivalent about sex as any preorgasmic housewife ever was. Men are finding that (a) having erections is not automatic, (b) sexual pleasure can be elusive, and (c) having the drive to "score" is not their birthright For some of them, coming out of the closet with their erotic alienation is a burden lifted from their balls. That burger is looking damn good.

The sensational event that has made so many unsatisfied men visible is the unbelievable sales of the erectile dysfunction drug Viagra. V was originally marketed to the Bob Doles of the world, the men over fifty who were finding the duration of their erection flagging for the first time. Older men hadn't exactly been boasting about this problem—it wasn't manly to admit it—but once they were offered a quick fix, they were voracious. They wanted to enjoy sex again the way they had in the past; they wanted to impress and please their partners; and they wanted to regain the youthfulness and masculinity symbolized by a hard, ready dick.

What's so interesting about Viagra is the number of pills being popped for performance enhancement, rather than erectile dysfunction. Viagra is being used like a one-night insurance policy, to create a facsimile of a porn-star experience. Men are aiming for sexual performance the way they *never* had it, a sensation they haven't felt since the time they were teenagers beating off in bed. These aren't men looking for youth, they're *youth* who, in the prime of their lives, have found sex with partners to be disappointing and even humiliating because their penises didn't "behave" the way they believe it's supposed to. The pleasure it afforded them seemed less than the hype has led them to expect.

Viagra is all about hype. The news headlines about Viagra have consistently seized upon the notion of the drug's abuse with scandals about how gay men were having parties with it, or that it was the Manhattan cocktail of choice, taken with a shot of tequila. Street-drug aficionados rejoiced that now there was finally something to reverse the limp effects of Ecstasy—by taking the white pill and the blue pill together, one can achieve both cosmic and carnal results.

I've witnessed the parties, the drug mixing and the celebratory air about the drug. But more poignant are the stories of the men I speak to who are using Viagra quite conservatively at home to please their partners, or the ones carrying it around with them like a condom, just in case. They aren't doing it for a thrill, they're using the drug to defend their reputations and meet their lovers' expectations. They know they're expected to produce wood, on contact and that it won't be pretty if they can't. They fear their lover will feel scorned and unappreciated, and the backlash might get ugly. This anxiety is what promotes their use of Viagra, not their search for ecstatic sex. Not a very erotic or romantic picture, to say the least.

Why is sex problematic for men now, when that kind of problem was women's burden in the past? I can only speculate, because the research simply isn't there. Sex research about men's erectile dysfunction is woefully inadequate—and Pfizer, Viagra's manufacturer, isn't sharing its trade insights. Instead, what we have is the gossip that has affected every American bedroom. Ask a single woman who's dating—at least dating men out of high school— and you're likely to get a story from her about how men aren't as sexually aggressive as they used to be. Ask a married woman, and you might hear from her about how they don't have sex at all without a dose of V in advance. And as for the porn industry—it's a rare day to meet a V-free actor these days.

The most alarming possibility as to why men are sagging is that something poisonous is in our water, or our air, or our food—take your pick. Anyone who watches the cancer epidemic we're living in, or who takes a look at dropping fertility rates, has had the distinct nightmare that the human race has ensured its own destruction by creating our own ecological putsch.

Then there's the sensitivity argument, which sounds like a silver lining: that men have had it with women's inane stereotypes about their bodies and minds. The truth is that men can be turned on without erections; they can achieve orgasm without a raging hard-on, and their emotions and minds are just as tied to their cock as any woman's is to her clit.

Many men are now openly exasperated with women thinking that they can be satisfied with a warm hole and a squeeze. Men appreciate their own sense of foreplay; they dream of being seduced; and they want to be treated like individuals between the sheets, instead of stroke-by-numbers cartoons.

Finally, there's the drug overload theory, which is the creepiest, yet most observable, trend of all. Thousands of men are taking antidepressants, and all those concoctions depress the libido. Prozac, Zoloft, Paxil, and all the rest have made a lot of men feel "content" at the expense of feeling horny. Desire, along with sadness, anger, and other deep feelings, doesn't feel so pressing anymore with the new mood levelers. Men who got rid of their depression have told me that they miss their sex drive, but they find their new contentment to be enough compensation. What saddens me is that a man would be asked to choose between his sexual passion and his will to live—one used to think of those emotions as being part of the same *joie de vivre*.

Advertisement Four:

A group of buddies have gathered at one member's house to watch the big football game. They don't know where their pal Doug is—he's late and they know him to be a true fan. Every one of these guys is in his thirties, with not a wrinkle or gray hair among them.

The story cuts to Doug, coming home with groceries and a bouquet of flowers in his arms. He busies himself about the house—making dinner, plumping pillows—to delight his wife, who steps in from work a few minutes later. She is utterly enchanted with him, and the music swells with their desire. A voice-over breaks in to tell us how many men don't realize what erectile dysfunction is, how common it is, and what can be done to treat it.

Meanwhile back at the football party, we see the dudes shaking their heads and worrying about Doug's no-show. But now we realize that this is not just a bunch of sports fans; this is a room of guys who haven't been laid in ages, and it's their decision to refrain from the marriage bed, not their wives'. Pfizer's name flashes on the T.V. screen, and the narrator encourages us to contact our physician and ask for details. The name Viagra is never mentioned.

There's no doubt about it: Young men are the new target for E.D. drugs and debates about men's sexual future. Masculine sex drives have been questioned before by all types of philosophers, but those intellectuals never dreamed that the future of men's sex lives was destined to be determined far more by medical and environmental means than by patriarchal means.

Men's declining sexual self-interest is disturbing. I never would have guessed that this would be the dilemma I'd be confronting thirty years after die modem sexual liberation movement began. I'm all for men being more sensitive and discriminating about their sexual state; but what I see in the sexual arena is that men feel disconnected from their bodies and from the dating game—and feel pessimistic about anything changing.

They take Viagra; they resent Viagra; they hide with Viagra. And like women who pine for an erotic revelation, they cherish romantic dreams of a Princess Charming- a lover whose innocent gaze and mind-reading touch would deliver them from their despair and disconnection. Until then, that bit of beef and that brew are looking better all the time.

OLD AND IN THE NUDE

LAST NIGHT I WENT to see one of my favorite actors, Harvey Fierstein, perform a one-man show at a performance festival in San Francisco. He warmed up the Bay Area crowd by telling nasty little jokes about Los Angeles:

"So this Beverly Hills woman goes to her plastic surgeon for her five hundredth collagen-lipo-tuck.

"He says to her, 'I'm sick of seeing you all the time. I'm going to put a key on top of your head, and every time you want another face-lift, you just reach under your hairpiece and give it a little twist.'

"A few months go by, and the lady shows up at the doctor's door again.

"'What are you doing here? Isn't the key working?' he cries.

"'Oh, yes, it worked wonderfully the first dozen times I tried it,' replied the lady. 'But now look at the *bags* under my eyes!'

"'Those aren't bags, sweetheart—those are your tits! And if you don't lay off, pretty soon you're going to have a beard!'"

Harvey got a big laugh, but my amusement was laced with more than a touch of anxiety.

Frankly, those women among us who still think of ourselves as "young" have no bloody idea what we're going to look like when we are unavoidably and undeniably old. For all we know, we *are* going to sport beards, and there's no telling where our tits are going to hang although the tumor is that it's going to be somewhere around our calves.

Shortly before my fortieth birthday, I attended a women's nudist retreat in Palm Springs, where I found myself one of the youngest members of the gathering. In case you haven't heard, "nude recreation" is one of the few booming parts of the travel industry, and there are a handful of resorts in Palm Springs that cater to just this sort of visitor. At such a clothing-optional spot, you get to sit around the pool, read your paper, play tennis, and gather 'round the barbecue—all without a stitch on. My favorite part is waking up in the morning and rolling out the door to get a cup of coffee without my bathrobe. It feels so healthy that, by check-out time, you actually feel indignant when you have to put on your clothes to get back in your car and join the rest of the overwrapped world.

I've been a hippie-style nudist since I was a teenager, enjoying the beach and hot tubs. But when you have a few extra pennies to visit one of these clothing-optional resorts, or to take one of the nude yacht vacations in the Caribbean, you enter a whole new lap of luxury. No more keeping an eye out for the police, or for voyeurs with cameras. There are playgrounds and spas, and even organized activities for kids, so you can take your whole family. You lie on a chaise lounge next to an Olympic-size pool, reading daydreaming ordering cocktails—all without covering up.

I belong to a clothing-optional club in the Santa Cruz Mountains called *Lupin*. It's part of a network of clubs across the county that form a counterpoint to the legislators, busy-bodies, and Puritans who each year try to figure out another way to criminalize and villainize nudity. To all the moralists, we give the classic nudist reply: "Yeah, you must be right—if God had wanted us to be nude, we would have been born that way."

At Lupin, I see a lot of naked people doing all the things that people do at a country club. It's also not particularly erotic. Nakedness only works as titillation until you get used to it, and that takes just a few hours in the daylight. At my retreat in Palm Springs, which is traditionally a retirement haven, the most interesting thing was to see how women's bodies actually age, and to imagine what's going to happen to mine.

I have been a little shy to share my findings. Does everyone else know what naked sixty-plus-year-old women's bodies look like? I don't think those *Playboy* spreads of Nancy Sinatra count—I'm talking realism here. When I was young I saw my mother undressed (she was young as well!) in the course of changing and bathing but that's only one example. I never see any mention of the subject in fashion magazines or interviews with veteran movie stars. Sure, someone will complain about their crow's-feet, but they're talking about the dainty little lines of a forty-year-old, not someone two decades older. At a certain point, you must reach an age at which you realize that all this pathetic gasping at the dewy-eyed beauty of an adolescent is beside the point and, furthermore, impossible to achieve. Then what?

My friend Betty Dodson, now in her seventies, has written volumes about sexuality for women. She told me that she has grown into a hugely satisfied dirty old lady. "When I walk down the street, no one notices me. It's as if I'm invisible—which, after a lifetime of being stared at and appraised, is kind of a gas. Now I'm staring at them. I ogle the good-looking ones as much as I want to. One time this little bike messenger caught on to what I was doing and he stepped right up to me: 'You ought to be ashamed of yourself!' Well, it's too late for that, buddy!"

I talked with several women in their sixties at the retreat, and when I asked them about their sex lives, I found to my surprise that their answers were ageless. Most of them enjoyed sex—by themselves, with a partner, or both. And for those who didn't, their reactions applied to their entire lives: Perhaps they'd never cared for lovemaking all that much, or found masturbation pointless. The way they *looked*—in shape or out of shape, made-up or plain-faced—had nothing to do with their answers or attitudes.

So let's talk about shape. The thing I noticed about all men and women past their forties is that their waistlines become more like a child's. You can be very skinny or roly-poly, but the differential between your chest, middle and hips becomes more subtle or, in some cases, irrelevant.

I knew from studying the human body that women's waists thicken after childbirth, and then later with aging. But I guess I fell for the hype that, if you were slender enough, you would always have a fetching indentation in your middle. Now I realize Miss Scarlett wasn't kidding you're going to need a corset and a strong Mammy to tie you up if this is the look you need to achieve.

My survey would not be complete if I didn't tell you what happens to your overall look if you were a patron of the plastic surgery arts in your middle age and have now reached elder-hood.

There were several women tanning in Palm Springs who, I noticed, had undergone tit and face jobs sometime in the past—after all, this practice has been going on for decades. Believe me, they stood out. The effect is like a real-life version of *Star Trek*. You know how, whenever there's an alien character, they look basically human but with a weird twist to the forehead, or an extra-exciting figure? When one part of your body is silicone, while the rest of you is responding to crepe and drape, the implant looks more theatrical than believable.

On the other hand, I can't get over how good most old people continue to look below the neck. One's face can be a prune; but further down, it's amazing how some people's skin can be so smooth and soft, their breasts full, their hips and thighs ready to rumba. Yes, gravity is definitely a player, but the face is the place that ages the most. I say, save the bucks on the plastic surgery and buy a lot of sun hats.

During our weekend, I became acquainted with one woman in her fifties who had a gorgeous tan body with little gold chains around her waist and neck, beautiful muscle tone—the whole bit. But on Sunday, when she put on a flowered frock, blazer, and sneakers, leaving only her face and hands exposed, she looked like Granny in *The Beverly Hillbillies*!

My conclusion: Older women are much sexier with their clothes off. Ready-to-wear fashions are doing older women worse than a disservice; they're an insult. This may be significant news for people who are shopping in their golden years. If you're looking for a lover and are over fifty, I suggest signing up for one of these nude cruises on the double—and get a couple of those pretty gold chains while you're at it.

PORNOGRAPHIC FUTURES

WHAT DO VICTORIA'S SECRET and inflatable sheep have in common? Twenty years from now, twenty-first century pornography is going to look like the last word in American mainstream advertising—not the artistic and bohemian success that many of its defenders long for, but rather the final operatic ring of the "Sex Sells" legend. We will indeed know that sex sells, but we will wonder whether sex gets it on anymore, or if it just dresses up and looks for the next sucker.

Porn started mainstreaming with the best of intentions, and the most improbable of proponents. Rogue feminists started selling vibrators in the 1970s, with clit power coursing through their fingertips. Thanks to them, the idea that women were uninterested in erotic shopping evaporated. Shopping lust won out over sexual fear—not a feminist revolution, but rather the victory of the Material Girl.

Old-school pornographers were presented with the challenge of "niche" salesmanship to two very different groups: the traditional raincoaters and the newly liberated ladies. At first the old guard fussed and moaned, but then they started counting the cash and realized this was rather remarkable after all. In the next two decades, the "butch" and "femme" of pornographic capitalism are going to explode and become as conforming in their appearance as Barbie and G.I. Joe.

How do porn-meisters look at the future of "women's erotica, "as it's so breathily whispered? The basic sales pitch is: Tempt the chicks with Victoria's Secret, then slip them a naughty storybook. Next, suggest a "tasteful" video, and before you know it, a matching compact and vibrator are in their handbag.

Was this what feminists had in mind for the Big Clit Revolution? No, most of the women who pioneered the erotic renaissance take one look at the cutesy sex boutiques for women and clutch their labryses. The femme sex bunnies can be as exasperating as cleavage-popping teen idols proclaiming "girl power!" when you know they wouldn't stick up for each other one week. They aren't sincere; they didn't sign on for the revolution, but rather for the matching accessories.

On the other hand, if the shopping-mall approach to erotica softens the female market by appealing to their just-wanna-please-my-man prejudices, those same customers-after they've had a screaming blue orgasm or two—may develop a more self-determined interest. That babe in line to buy a strap-on dildo and an economy-size bottle of lube probably started out reading *Cosmo* under her covers one night a long long time ago. The female orgasm remains deeply subversive, so in that rosy light, there's hope for the idealistic and rebellious.

The traditional audience for smut—who are experiencing the first politically incorrect revival of their existence—are the tried-and-true porn dogs, the teenage boys growing hair on their palms from masturbating and the guilty husbands hiding their porn stash in a fish-tackle box. Our porn forefathers have thoroughly studied these sorts of men, and have basically nailed their needs down to the floor. This is an audience who wants poppin' fresh starlets sucking and fucking and they are not much motivated to explore any major innovations. They may dip into a fetish video or two, but they are sated by bottled blonde meat and potatoes day in and day out.

What's new for boys and girls is the censor-free breakthrough of the Internet, which has spawned a fetish market that literally has to be gawked at to be believed. Propriety in the mainstream media has always suppressed the kinky and the raw. We never even got to imagine about what lay beyond the hard blue line. Now the Internet has opened Pandora's box, and fetish is king. You see the effects of fringe sex at every level of erotic photography.

Take, for example, one trend *du jour:* bug-squashing. By the time you read this, I'm sure it will be passé, but that is a trend's nature: today's extreme is tomorrow's sentimental toast.

This morning as I pen this essay, however, bug-squashing—or "crushing" as it's nicknamed—is a hot item. Take a look at some of the porn sites devoted to women in dominatrix gear, with six-inch spike heels, who grind their stilettos into various squishy things: cockroaches, slabs of meat, and of course, male genitalia.

"What is the point?" you may exclaim—but that's like asking children what's the point of sticking beans up their noses.

There are, of course, a few people who consistently get off on foot fetishism—on squishing critters and diabolical high heels—but they are the minority of viewers for these images. The most popular reason for people to click on and download crusher porn is pure carnival amusement—what I call pornographic rubbernecking.

The point of rubbernecker pornography is sensation. The gain is a physical jolt: the fresh moment when you were once intact but are now spread open in visceral response You can quickly move onto smirking and scoffing but, nevertheless, your first gasp was real.

The most bizarre image you can find on the Internet quickly morphs its way to the general public's view, particularly through the fashion world, which has been taking cues from porn for almost fifty years. A refined version of the "deadly stiletto" theme—a perfect white foot in a spectacular shoe, grinding into a man's hand—can be found in a Louis Vuitton leather ad in the issue of *Vogue* on my coffee table. Other fashion and sex connoisseurs will remember the famous Calvin Klein campaign where sulking teenage models posed in crappy little fake-wood paneled dens to simulate seventies stroke mags.

Rubbernecker websites and videos will increasingly be the clarion call of our erotic future, much to the outrage of conservatives and the disdain of intellectuals.

Wanna see someone pee on an expensive oriental rug? Stretch their labia lips a yard wide? Dress like a horny terrorist? How about a bearded she male wrestling in an iron chastity belt?

Even if you disconnect entirely, someone is bound to create a diluted version of all these things for consumption in *The New Yorker*—at a much higher price—before the day is up.

It's a sad new version of an old question: What happened to the fighting spirit of rock 'n' roll? What happened to a sexual liberation that would turn gender relations on their head? How did we get from smashing monogamy to squishing caterpillars? I can only surmise that sensationalism goes hand in hand with taboo breaking. The public is preoccupied with infantile fixations, like babies who thoroughly examine the contents of their diapers before they are able to leave them behind. If they can buy their way into a reckless taste of the forbidden, they will. Our culture is saddled with the sexual fears and prejudices of a titillated, high-strung three-year-old.

Sure, I'm disappointed. But I take the long view: If we could just get over this hump, the novelty acts will leave center stage. The worst thing that could happen to erotica at this point would be Internet regulation, or conforming to the standards of the mainstream broadcasters. If we stop the parade of the weird and the banal, we will go right back to the starting block, another generation stuck in repression's playpen.

 If only we could just stomach "Anything Goes!" for a couple decades, maybe we could "Move On,"as they say. After you've seen it all, don't you yearn to reexamine the basics, to refresh your imagination with less shock and more self-reflection? We have never had one genuine break from our heritage of sexual dishonesty and erotic hucksterism. If it boggles our minds, it's only because the true future of erotica is, unfortunately, unimaginable to us all.

VARGAS IN DRAG

ONCE UPON A TIME there was a pinup girl, a whore with a heart of gold who realized she could line her pockets with a little well-placed advertising. She was an exhibitionist, proud of her assets; or, in another view, she was under pressure to exploit her physical charms, regardless of pride or joy. She wanted to be an actress, a showgirl, maybe even a star. In real life, she might never have made it past dime-a-dance.

But something happened to the pinup girl: She got religion, which in the case of the American World War II effort, was nothing but righteously devout patriotism. Whatever a soldier wanted or needed to fight the Nazis became sacred. If he wanted pictures of beautiful babes to masturbate and pray to, by God, who wouldn't support democracy?

The pinup girl put on a uniform, and she hitched it up good and tight. She showed that she was not only a tiger in the sack, but a hellion on a missile, a bombardier Amazon. Her sexual charisma was just part of her winning attitude, and with her inspiring image, a warrior could feel as if nothing would defeat him. She had *arrived*.

Today, if you travel America, you will find little boys playing soldier, not with plastic army men, but with outrageously graphic video games. In each fight-to-the-death scenario, the boys must pick who their "character" will be—the persona they both identify with and give combat instructions to. These little boys don't know who pinup artist Vargas was; they weren't even born during the pinup heyday. They don't know that Alberto Vargas (Americanized to "Varga") created the drawings of comely girls in men's magazines that have inspired every centerfold and cartoon buxom-bunny since Witness the über-femme who would be blissfully at home in any 1940s Vargas

Mommy's Little Girl

Girl gatefold: Lara Croft, *Tomb Raider* heroine and kick-ass sex-symbol superstar.

Vargas's girls, his wartime divas, set the course for modem pinup girls. He liberated them from bordello advertising and transformed them into all-American girls. Yet their wholesomeness and mainstream acceptance came at an ironic cost: the pinup girl lost quite a bit of her devoted femininity. Vargas's women may have floated about in bits of diaphanous lingerie, but many of them were built like boy soldiers with bosoms. They wear lots of makeup, and they have lots of attitude, but they also have no hips, and show no intention of fainting. Sure, there'd been tough girls in our feminine imagery before, but they weren't glorious like this—triumphant, winning without breaking a nail.

Today there is no sexual heroine on the horizon who isn't a diva warrior. Whether it's Xena, Warrior Princess, or Pamela "Don't-Call-Me-Babe" Anderson, live-action erotic heroines are warriors first and lovers later—if you're among the lucky chosen. Sure, they live to inspire, but for all the erections they promote, they also lend an air of invincibility. You not only want to seduce these Valkyries, you want to become them, and that's as true for little boys as it is for little girls.

My interest in the Vargas pinup collection comes from my curiosity about the moment in time when "the girl in the picture" became sexually assertive, transgressing the indolent feminine caricatures that once defined the erotic female portrait. This postwar, postcorset pinup girl is not round; she is not propped up with pillows; she is not waiting for something to happen to her. She expresses her lust and humor with unladylike independence—she even broods without apology. By Lara Croft's standards, the Vargas Girl is just a slip of a thing but then, Ms. Croft's caricature has never been emblazoned on an A-bomb either, so maybe she still has something to learn.

In looking over the Vargas catalog of pinups, the likenesses that stand out the most to my transgression-seeking eye are the ones in which Vargas's girls turn boyish—in male costume, physique, pose, and expression. Most of these are not the famous peep-through-the-nightie portraits that became so ubiquitous in Vargas's *Playboy* era, but are rather his strongest patriotic expressions of the war period—and express his cosmopolitan fantasy life, playing footsie with American puritanism.

An illustrated version of this story is available with all the color reproductions, at: http://tinyurl.com/susie-vargas/.

In the May 1941 gatefold, we see a striking example of the latter a Thanksgiving-style Pilgrim, smoking her cigarette in a see-through black gown, apparently giving a line to a Spanish *maja,* clad in white lace and looking rather unconcerned in her own private daydream. The decidedly uncontrite Puritan is smirking and flicking her ash. In my imagination, I could hear the Pilgrim witch delivering a punch line to the Papist babe about some poor sucker she just put through the wringer. What we have to be thankful for, indeed!

The September 1947 calendar girl also lends herself to a particularly relevant interpretation by the standards of today's erotic icons. In this image, unlike any other, the model is slouched, smoking hiding her eyes, not in shyness but in private sulking. Her cold shoulder overwhelms her Vargas bust-line for once, both figuratively and literally. Her hair is not immaculate; it's unkempt and falling down, curling around her strong upper arm. Below the knees, however, we see a strangely different woman—lower legs posed on command ("porno toes," I call them), with the model flexing the arch of her feet to achieve Barbiesque high heels.

When I first contemplated this particular Vargas Girl, I was visiting her on my Internet browser. Due to the size of my screen,

I could only view the upper half of her body without scrolling. I was so struck by her internal point of view, her I-don't-give-a-damn posture, that it was many minutes before I scrolled down to her paper-doll legs—which, at that point, looked like an aberration.

Vargas clearly took a risk with this internal, rebellious portrayal; and for some reason, through lack of craft or determination, he didn't pursue her body language down to the floor. I prefer to contemplate her personality as it is most forcefully expressed in her face and upper body.

What makes this Vargas redhead so sexy by today's standards is that she captures the current erotic principles of rebellion, melancholy, and self-centeredness. These qualities are the very spirit of everything in hip titillation, from *Rebel Without a Cause* to rock 'n' roll itself. Today's sex symbols are not wholesome or well-scrubbed—and neither is this little witch. She seems to be unavailable not because she's too good for you, but because she's too bad for her own bad self. Like any MTV siren of today, she is not so terrifying to others as she is potentially self-destructive. Our modem culture has a sexual ache for an Achilles' heel, and that's exactly what we should have seen at the bottom of this angel's limbs, instead of a perky pedicure.

Vargas had either a schizophrenic or a lackadaisical attitude toward rendering a holistic, complete female figure. His pinups seem to lose their resolve halfway through their expression so often that they remind me of ancient rediscovered statues who are missing an arm.

Take the gatefold from December 1942, for example an adorable Santa Claus specialty, with a full-cheeked, robust redhead laughing gaily at her holiday surprise Her arm looks as if she works on a farm, or drives a big rig—you almost expect to see her CB handle in a caption underneath. From the bust up, this gal is strong with some weight to both her chuckle and her physique.

Below that proud bosom, however, her body is taken over by something else—a wasp waist, an invisible bottom, and the template legs that we saw facing the other direction in September 1947. What was the force that spun Vargas in two directions; was it as banal as a lack of skill or time or was it a tempest of wills between artist and publisher?

The feminine ass is something that has to be considered further in Vargas's pinups. In some, though not all of his paintings, the women simply haven't achieved that secondary feminine characteristic—their buttocks are like those of a fabulous boy. He created these images long before Twiggy, anorexia, or Kate Moss, so we can't blame it on the trends of the time, which favored a more womanly, hip-centric view.

The most shocking and transparent example of this "boy with boobs," the Vargas pinup in drag is the June 1942 gate-fold, which features a muscular, broad-shouldered blonde, nude except for a ridiculous sun hat hiding his/her slim hips. Take away the bonnet and the profile of the breast, and you have a dead ringer for one of George Platt Lyon's sailor boys photographed from the back—Lyon was the master of homo-erotic WWII-era photography.

February 1942's calendar page, a court jester in red, is another boy/girl whose feminine attributes disappear as you step away from it—or, in my case when I simply take off my glasses. The breasts and stomach are curiously "stuck" in the middle of the figure, and they seem to have no effect on the silhouette. Is she getting ready to play a gender trick on the court with her magic mandolin?

Mommy's Little Girl

Vargas's girls explore a full closet of male costume: the jester, sailor, weight lifter, soldier, hunter, classical composer, cowboy with six-shooters, and the father of our county. My favorite of these drag portraits is the August 1942 drawing of the defiant George Washington! This time Vargas delivers a completely feminine physique that takes over the presidency and dares you to do anything about it. Her swagger and her cape thrown to one side give the air of a pirate crossed with the Marquis de Sade. She's a dominatrix, she "WANTS YOU" to service her *and* serve the country with equal obedience.

In general, however, Vargas in drag leans more toward Peter Pan than the magnificent Daddy/Diva-ness of the George Washington centerfold. In the October 1941 calendar, we see an archer, bracing her bow skyward, with her impressive aim and strength somewhat diminished by the silly pair of elf shoes on her feet. What is it with Vargas and his women's legs betraying their heads? This Diana should have been in boots; we should have seen her target. This tomboy could have been a contender.

Whether posing with weapons or laughing on the floor while she counts her push-ups, the Vargas Girl was an Olympian—jockeying for position, laughing at risk, sporting unflappable confidence. Aside from the phenomenon of Babe Didrikson Zaharias, the female athletic giants of Vargas's heyday simply didn't appear on the American pop-culture map. If they ever made an appearance, they were sure to be called lesbians.

Maria Elena Buszek, a Vargas scholar, has written that "Vargas's anatomical exaggerations of the female figure would have been downright monstrous on a real woman." But if you picked the right night in Hollywood, Vargas Girls would not so much have been sci-fi apparitions as they would have been dyke-baited—or, better yet, recruited as she-male porn stars. By today's standards, Vargas Girls are gender-benders.

Among Vargas's curious gender-bending drawings, none is more romantic and female sympathetic than that of his July 1943 gatefold of a bridal kiss, between a groom in uniform and his veiled beloved. This soldier groom has not one whisker on his cheeks. His lids are darkened, with eyelashes as thick as a girl's. His face recalls no one so much as Elizabeth Taylor, at the moment she kissed Montgomery Clift in *A Place* **in the Sun**. In the famous still of this embrace from George Cukor's film, Taylor's eyes were also downcast, her lips yearning for the reckoning that can be viewed just as clearly in the Vargas bridal portrait. The only difference is that Montgomery Clift, young and fair as he was, was still a hundred times more masculine than the groom in Vargas's chapel.

My first reaction to this wedding-day gatefold was that it was the perfect retro-bliss poster to promote same-sex marriages, in this case of an exquisite butch/femme lesbian couple. Indeed, the blonde femme in this portrait is the one with the more determined jaw, her mouth suggesting a hint of sadness or even cruelty. Her ambivalence, with her mouth still not accepting her lover's, creates even more dissonance and attraction.

The contemporary craze for pinup girls and their subversive possibilities began in the eighties, when rebellious feminists, particularly lesbians and bisexual women, looked for visual role models who seemed to offer transgressive potential. If Bettie Page could be simultaneously an athlete, bathing beauty, and Bondage Princess; if Katharine Hepburn and Greta Garbo could vamp it up in slacks and a devil-may-care attitude, pinups offered a catalyst for fantasy material to adventurous women who wanted all the sexual power they could afford.

In the 1980s, Vargas's pinups were reimagined by a popular artist, Olivia de Bernardinis, whose line of prints, greeting cards, and calendars all deified the conquering femme with a direct line to the Vargas gatefold imagery. This time, however, there was no patriotism involved, just sheer sex. This time, a female artist held the brush. As someone who was involved in the retail end of "wimmin's" culture at the time, I can well recall the stampede of women eager to collect every image of de Bemardinis's work. Men coveted them as well; but this time, women were the new audience, not simply looking to imitate the model's clothes, but to cherish her eroticism, to be aroused and inspired by the knowledge that a woman was the author of these fantasies.

What would Vargas think today of Olivia de Bernardinis, or photographers Del LaGrace, Annie Sprinkle, Phyllis Christopher, Morgan Gwenwald—the host of radical women artists who have taken the pinup to new heights of queer romance and genderfuck distinctions?

How would he cope with Lara Croft, raiding the identities of boys and men alike on a small-screen battleground? Would he hide behind a polka-dot sun hat, shying away from the spotlight of the new sexual authenticity? Or would he face us down, like George Washington with tits and ass, defying us ever to diminish his legend?

STILL INSATIABLE

I TOTALLY FELL FOR IT. When the package arrived with a hand-printed message scrawled prankishly on the envelope, my hands shook a little. It said, "A letter from your *first* girlfriend!" My heart skipped a beat No way—was it really her, after twenty-plus years?

The last time I heard from my first girlfriend, we were in high school. Or at least I was; she was about to drop out. She walked down my front steps with my green metallic flake motorcycle helmet, which she promised she was just "borrowing." She got on the back of a motorcycle with some idiot I didn't spare the time to look at, and I never saw her again. I was going to some commie potluck and she was on her way to the Ontario Motor Speedway. This was the girl who taught my tongue what to do in an open-mouthed kiss, who dropped acid with me for the first time, who cursed in French, and could get my new kittens to do her every bidding. A letter from her would make me faint.

But no, this package was from a different kind of girlfriend, a sex symbol who was just as much of a trigger for my teenage nostalgia, but whom I had never met in person. Inside this envelope was a video and comeback announcement from none other than the best-selling actress in the history of porn, Marilyn Chambers. The video is called *Still Insatiable*.

I wonder how many Americans today have an instant mental image when Marilyn Chamber's name is mentioned. Do you flash on her fucking in a trapeze from *Behind the Green Door*, being taken by all comers—or are you haunted by her voracious sexual marathon on a pool table in the original *Insatiable?* For most people, even if they never saw a hard-core film in their lives, Marilyn Chambers is that sweet young thing with the adorable smile cradling her baby on the Ivory Snow detergent box. This is Chamber's legacy—the girl who went from soap model to porn star legend, cast in the first movie that defined hard-core (*Green Door*) as well as the most popular adult film of all time *(Insatiable).*

Reading the publicist's letter for *Insatiable 2,* I learned that in recent years Marilyn had no interest in ever making a hardcore movie again, because of her concerns about AIDS. She is a mom, and like any older parent, she's in to long-term preservation. Maybe that was all baloney, but it sounded like a good excuse for a pronounced absence. When VCA, the releasing company behind her comeback, began their procondom policy, she had second thoughts. Her good friend Veronica Hart, from the seventies, porno's golden years, offered to direct a video that would show off Chambers to her best advantage, and they decided to go for it.

Marilyn, of course, has grown up from when she was a whippet-slim fox with a boyish figure. She's womanly now, with breasts, hips, and Victoria's Secret corsets. I asked Hart how fans reacted to her comeback image, and she said, "About half are just irate because they don't ever want to see Marilyn again if she's not exactly as they remember. The other half wouldn't care *what* she looked like as long as they know it's her—they love her, period."

"I think I'm part of that last crowd," I said. What gave me goose bumps in the new video was when her steely blue eyes turned right into the camera, and that smile of hers made everything else in the picture disappear. Finally, a movie star who didn't ruin her face with Botox and a knife. She still looks like Marilyn. I never realized until now that that grin of hers, her instant expression of earthy satisfaction, is like Huck Finn, Miss America, and the first great fuck you ever had, all rolled into one.

When Marilyn made her first movie, neither she nor anyone else had any idea she was making history. Her early producers were just grateful to have a hot young girl who would go for it I don't think anyone realized what her star power was really all about: that captivating smile of hers personified a whole damn attitude about taking your pleasure and loving every minute of it. She has the same kind of charisma in her grin that gave Cary Grant an endless career.

The other key to Marilyn's appeal, the character behind that great face, is found in the title that most know her by: *Insatiable.* Although seventies pornophiles wouldn't have used this term, she could "bottom" like no one else I might even call her the prototype for the whole notion of "topping from below." She's an erotic masochist who wants to run the fuck.

Even though Chambers didn't make S/M or fetish movies per se, she could take an otherwise vanilla situation and turn it into a power-charged *tour de force*. I don't know what the male consensus on Marilyn Chambers is, but if you ask any woman who was affected by her early performances, they will tell you that her impact was in the way she grabbed you in that aggressive, yet submissive fantasy place—where you could imagine taking on the entire Marine Corps and then taunting them for more She was sassy and demanding, but the payoff was total vulnerability and ecstasy. I used to dream about being like her, feeling that open, being "made" to do things and loving it. Now, as I talked with Veronica Hart, I realized that my over-forty fantasies have turned the tables: now I know exactly what Marilyn wants, and I'd love to be the one to give it to her.

For some seventies nostalgia addicts, Susan Dey from *The Partridge Family* may be enough. But my retro-heart belongs to that girl who still hasn't returned my emerald green metal-flake helmet, and the porno goddesses I watched open-mouthed from the seats of an air-conditioned Pussycat Theater on a hot Anaheim afternoon. I'd welcome a comeback visit from either of them.

DIRTY BOOKSTORE DOCENT

MY NEIGHBOR, Linda, has returned home from a daunting first trip to an "adult novelty" store with her boyfriend, Terry. She was shaken and slightly chilled, but her sense of humor was still intact. She is not the sort of person to let her libido be destroyed by a retail nightmare, even if it was triple X-rated.

"What is with these places?" she demanded, stretching her hands a yard apart to illustrate her complaint.

"The first thing we saw when we came in was this gruesome rubber prick—*this* big! Who the hell uses that? And all the videos! Every cover looks the same. They're hideous, and all the titles are like, *Double-D Anal Ball Busters.*"

I told Terry, 'I don't think so!' When we finally left and went back to the car, some guy comes up to me in the parking lot and asks us if we want to join him for wife swapping. I mean, he was very polite, but the whole time I felt like I was a moving target!"

I shook my head like a disappointed high school principal.

"I can't believe you didn't ask me to chaperone you the first time," I said. "Going to these places is like visiting a museum—you need a history lesson, a decoder ring and an experienced docent if you want to have a clue as to what's really going on."

Linda collapsed on my sofa. "Well, you can start the debriefing now."

"There are things in that shop that you would probably like," I said, "but stores like the one you visited are like a 1960s time tunnel. They date back to the classic age of men's smoke shops—the ones with a room in the back that sold condoms and naughty nudist magazines. They aren't 'sex-positive.' They don't know feminism from a ball-busted hole in the ground. They're more like carny shows where you get a twenty-inch dong to stare at instead of a bearded lady. Every sex shop in America was like this until feminists started selling vibrators in the seventies. It's only been in the last decade that all these old farts realized that there was a new market to exploit, if they could just get over their raincoater attitude."

Unfortunately, Linda and I live in a small town which, despite being "nuclear-free," is still zoned to keep its one adult bookstore on the edge of town, far away from the respectable shops and malls. Our X-rated anachronism is called Frenchy's—and, needless to say, there is nothing "French" about it.

Frenchy's seems to be the quintessential adult bookstore name, a legacy from the eighteenth century and, later, the notion of naughty postcards from Paris.

When I was a college student in Santa Cruz in the eighties, there was still a local blue law that said that such retailers had to stock a certain percentage of nonsexual items. When you entered Frenchy's in those days, the racks in front were filled with dusty fishing and hunting guides of uncertain age, followed by less-well-lit shelves stocked with the real business: dirty books and magazines.

Nowadays, however, Frenchy's advertises its wares openly in the town's weekly liberal newspaper; it invites couples to come in for "fun," and it shelves its sexual merchandise up front. I wonder what happened to those now-classic fishing magazines.

Frenchy's thinks it has entered the modem era of sex-novelty merchandising. Most of the store, however, remains "old

school"——old boys' school to
women (and uninitiated me
inside.

People who want sex toys and
order or Internet shopping th
Toys in Babeland. These are
by females with a sunny dispo
proach to videos, and Westing
ing appliances.

But sometimes you have no ch
overnight delivery. That's whe
the glass-filled parking lot of t
building in town, right next
with the broken neon light bli

Entrez, you little Frenchy-seeke

First, let's dispense with the m
greet you as you walk through
lent of stone lions guarding die
New York Public Library. Rubb
mascots of the masculine world

When you see gigantic stone
cient artifacts, you don't excla
them for?" Nor should you here
these elephantine hoses for any
there to set the scene, to intimi
cate. Now, some people will w
buy these monsters for anal sex,
terments of the average homos
people (of any sexual orientation)
vices for anything more than a l
of a pin.

Next, there
infuriating
covers with
draw their

The numbe
are nothing
staring at t
ful about
cover may

The aesthe
tent. Adul
style of bo
They spen
movie. Th
people wil
tions. The

For this re
work you'
kind of cin
ing a movi
see a direct
has a follo
want to c
Blake ling
Ho-Hos a
them bot

You may
viewing
up closet
minutes
that the

are the mysteries of the video display. I agree, it's
that the box covers are so generic—mirror-shiny
photos of big titties, gaping holes, and tides that
spiration from the World Wrestling Federation.

one thing you must remember is that the covers
but illusion. You won't turn into a pillar of salt
em, but neither will you learn anything meaning-
hat's inside the box. The models you see on the
ot even appear in the movie.

ics of the box cover have little to do with the con-
distributors notice trends in the sales of a certain
, and they copy it madly to use for all their tides.
more on the box design than they do on the entire
y know that because porn isn't discussed in public,
have no reviews to go on, no personal recommenda-
box cover is the shill running the show.

son, to know the reputation of a porn director whose
e considering is more important than with any other
ma. Porn is a field where the auteur tradition of brand-
e with a personal vision is very much alive. If you even
r's name on a box cover, that means that this person
ving a fan base. That's a good sign. You certainly don't
nfuse a Max hardcore wall-banger with an Andrew
rie fantasia. It's like the difference between chocolate
d Beluga caviar—the same person is unlikely to love
.

want to preview some videos in one of the private
ooths at the back of the store—that's the little stand-
with a screen where you feed in quarters to look a few
t a time This is fun to try, but you need to understand
iewing booths are also not all that they appear.

The main reason the booths exist is not to provide dose viewings of upcoming features. No, these American architectural phenomena of space and darkness are for masturbating in a "secret place" with other men dose by. The hottest action isn't on the screen, it's the real guys cruising other real guys, each with a resolutely straight facade.

These men wouldn't be caught dead in a gay bar—in fact, they don't think of themselves as "gay" at all, not with the lifestyle connotations that word implies. They are attracted to the twilight zone of sexual identity offered by the peep shows: the chance for an illicit encounter with an anonymous and appropriately butch fellow traveler. They're not supposed to be having sex back in the booths of course—there's always the imminent threat of being busted—but that time-honored risk is part of the thrill.

If you are a woman entering the booths, most of the men will be pissed that you are mining the all-male atmosphere, and they will try to scare you away. A few of them will think you're a curiosity item and that you might be up for some hanky-panky. Either way, don't take it personally. They'll leave you alone if you're perfectly frank about what you're up to. You should speak at a normal volume. Laugh! Point! Go on at length! Any ordinary conversation is like a wet blanket in these joints where all communication is kept at the grunting level, and eye contact is everything.

Booth trolls are there to have sex. The vast majority aren't junkies, serial killers, or whatever other stereotypes leap to mind about those who buy butt plugs in public These guys want to get off—period—and they're there either because they don't feel as if there's any other place where that's allowed, or because they find the closet-case environment terribly sexy. The latter don't want Frenchy's ever to change. They don't want to talk to a cheery dyke in a warm room with flowers on the desk and strap-ons in every color. They want sex to be "bad," because they're afraid that the alterative is even worse than bad, it's banal. *Chacun à son gout*—as they might say at Frenchy's if they could stop mumbling for a minute.

For my own satisfaction, I like a dark secret place as much as anyone, but I am not paying extra for sexual guilt. I want my vibrator to run, my movies to speak to me, and my dildo sized to perfection. I will take my erotic business elsewhere, and I'm sure my neighbor and her boyfriend will follow me. Let Frenchy's be preserved as an odd piece of American sexual *puritanica backlashicus,* a giant pickle in a dusty jar.

HOW MUCH WOOD?

THE FIRST TIME I EVER WROTE about pornography, in the mid-eighties, I was the "X-Rated Screen Advisor" for *Penthouse Forum* magazine. What a popular feature it was: I received so many letters inquiring about pornographic etiquette and ethics, it would've kept Miss Manners occupied for years. The questions ranged from, "Who was that girl with the beautiful crossed green eyes who did the double penetration in a movie that started with an 'F'? to, "Can you recommend erotica for the very, very shy?"

There was one question, though, that came in the mailbox almost every week: "I am a guy who would like to be in a porn movie. How do I get *in?*"

"Getting in" is indeed the operative question. Not in the lecherous context of getting into the porn starlet's panties, but rather how to get into the extremely small, elite, and testy world of the men who walk the X-rated line, the actors known as Woodsmen.

There are thousands of women who have starred on the erotic screen since hard-core debuted in the early 1970s; but in all that time, there are actually only about a dozen men who have appeared repeatedly in straight porn film and video making. Of those who came into the scene in the early days many had theatrical training, movie careers—veteran porn stud/producer Paul Thomas still makes me smile when I see him in his old role as John the Baptist in *Jesus Christ Superstar*.

All these men came into the industry thinking that it sounded like a blast to have sex with pretty girls on camera. But the reason they stayed was more because they found an unusual gift in themselves—which, by real-life standards, might rather be considered a disability. A porn star cannot roll his eyes back in his head and get all soft and squishy thinking about pretty girls. He is expected to achieve his hard-ons on cue, over and over again, maintaining his nut until the director calls for his ejaculation. Male porn performance is about discipline to the camera—about cutting yourself off from outside influences to the point of being a relative emotional outsider to the sexual experience, more inside your own world than anyone else's.

This kind of body-mind control is something that men in other professions can completely identify with—professional sports for one, military training for another. But while those men are waging banks that may seem like metaphors for cocksmanship, it's not their actual penises doing the work. In other words, "getting wood" is a strange gig—not for everyone, and not always the most pleasant way to get laid. Those who stick with it need to enjoy the camaraderie and pressure of the porn world, thrive on the sexual variety, and of course, get a great deal of creative and erotic satisfaction from having people watch you fuck.

The other bottom-line qualification, besides single-minded exhibitionism, is that you need be a master of masturbation. I'm talking about a guy who can successfully beat off under extreme time constraints, with or without ill-fitting condoms, reciting baseball scores in his head, or talking to his mother about her broken radiator on the telephone Nerves of steel equal balls of steel.

One thing however, has changed the porn entrance exam for the average guy. In today's boom of amateur video, where any guy with a camcorder may be marketing the new top-ten sensation, the easiest way to get in a porn movie is to make it yourself.

The final strategy for landing a job as a porn actor is pure dumb luck, which is exactly what happened a month ago to an ex-lover (and good pal) of mine Jack has never done more than have a daydream about being a porn stud—and for that matter, he's daydreamed about being a fireman and the POTUS, too. But Jack got invited by a mutual friend, Shar Rednour, to be cast in her new porn movie. She gave him one week's notice, and he accepted on the spot: "This is something no forty-year-old man can turn down."

Why did Shar ask Jack, a total porno virgin? "He's part of our tribe; I can trust him," was her first reason.

"And he's got a pretty cock," was her second explanation, which I couldn't resist asking more about. "How would you know, Shar, being that you're a lifetime lesbian?"

"I don't know," she said, "Maybe I'm dreaming but I actually think dykes are more objective about this sort of thing!"

Jack, meanwhile, felt fine about how his penis would look on camera, but he was a little worried about everything else "Whoever heard of a middle-aged man making his *debut* in a porn movie?" he asked me, looking a little dazed. "In the beginning I said yes right away, 'cause it was like someone asking, 'Do you want to fly to Hawaii? Do you want to win a thousand dollars?' But now I wonder, what the hell am I doing?"

Jack told me his apprehensions while simultaneously filling out the required HIV-test forms for the movie and a new grant proposal application for the local hospital where he works— he's a social worker in his day job.

"Do you think anyone in the ER is ever going to see me in this flick?" he wondered. "Do they need to be forewarned?"

"It's the 'fore' part that's tricky," I said. "It would be one thing if you were striking a redemption pose and confessing that you once made a blue movie as a youth. But whoever heard of being *pre-demptive?*— 'By the way, everyone, I'm going to make a fuck film a few weeks from now; I'll need a personal day off.'"

Jack decided to go the time-honored route of employing discretion and a stage name, but to offer no apologies if asked. "It's one thing to be pro-erotica in theory," he said, "That's been easy all my life. But someone actually has to put their body on the line and take some pride in making something new and different." Thank you, Mr. President!

Onto the next topic: What should he do to prepare his body? A week before the shoot, he called me to ask, "Should I hit the tanning beds? Dye the gray? Pluck my nose hairs? Wax my ass?"

"Would it kill you to moisturize?" I said. "You need to ask your director," I went on, "but if you're not used to major beauty treatments, a week's notice is not a good time to begin."

I started to imagine some of the consequences. "One false step with the Grecian Formula, and you could look like Count Dracula by Saturday. I think you should calm down. You have a great body, and after all, when it comes to comparisons, all you have to think is two words: 'Ron Jeremy.'"

We talked about the hard-on question, too. Jack was more relaxed about his cock than his gray hair. After all, he rationalized; it's only one time, a small low-key production. What Jack was more worried about was how he'd get on with his scene partner, a professional named Chloe, who's won every prize in the adult entertainment industry—an actual superstar.

"The one thing that would turn me off," Jack said, "would be if she rejected, me—if she were cold or hostile."

"Oh, c'mon, you're paranoid from watching too many Traci Lords biographies," I said. Like most porn stars, Chloe will probably be a working-class tomboy with a big family and the ole 'can-do' spirit. She wants to like you; she wants to look good. Unless she thinks you thrive on disdain, she's not going to play that card."

Would Jack and Chloe find true wood? Jack was green-lighted by the director, based on the entirely unproven belief that Jack could provide erections for their camera at the crack of a starting board. But could he actually do it? We laughed a lot about what comeuppance he might deserve for his boasting; but truly, I hoped that he could enjoy this unorthodox version of having his dreams come true

To prove my good will for the project, I volunteered to provide craft services to the entire crew while they were in town to shoot Jack and Chloe's scenes. When I went to the bagel store to pick up my order the first morning, the waitress smiled brightly and asked, "Are you off to a picnic?"

"No," I said, "I'm off to a porn shoot! The talent needs bread! "

Jack's scene required him to "show wood" in the following order: first, they wanted to see Chloe penetrating him anally with a dildo in a harness. Then they wanted him to have vaginal intercourse with her, and finally, bumfuck her for the grand finale.

Jack said that he doubted he would be hard when she was fucking him, although he was sure it would feel good. He speculated he might even have an orgasm while semisoft. "When I'm getting fucked like that, it feels like I have a giant clit that's getting rubbed all over from behind." Yes, it all sounds very nice—but could Mr. Feelgood rebound out of the big clit afterglow and sport a hard-on for the next sequence?

The day before the shoot, Jack spent some time talking to Chloe about the business, and how she likes to work. "She says I'm V-free, "he said, like he's just gotten an 'A' in chemistry." That means I'm performing without using Viagra; I'm old school. Only the veterans work without Viagra now, the young ones are just popping pills. Chloe says she likes men who are V-free because it's the way she can tell she's doing her job."

Wow, there's the end of a dynasty, I thought. Now anyone can be a porn stud—another elite destroyed by technology.

Chloe was nice, down to earth, just like I thought, and much smaller than Jack. She has a body like a ballerina, which is exactly what she was trained for, years before her current life in the sex business. I've noticed that a lot of women athletes, and professional dancers, have come to work in porn. It's not just their body types, it's their stamina as well, their custom of competition—as well as the "no pain, no gain" attitude of pushing yourself past the limit. If you saw Chloe in real life, you might be tempted to coddle her with chocolate milkshakes and cheeseburgers; she's skinny. But on film or video, she looks curvier; it's that photogenic miracle where curvaceousness springs to life on camera from the right kind of bone structure.

Jack agonized over his physique for the opposite reason. He looks like a jock in real life—this is the kind of guy who thinks a 5K run before breakfast sounds like fun—but in pictures, he is, as the director put it, "Thick." She said it with butch praise in her voice, as a nod to his masculinity and strength. But Jack groaned. "Great, I'm going to look like some fat gorilla devouring this little girl!"

Jack was reassured that there were ways to make everybody look fetching. This movie was designed to be a slice of life, starring all amateurs—aside from Chloe. The rest of the couples in the video were volunteers, and what they wanted to do on camera could probably have not been dreamed up by any screenwriter.

One of the other actors in the movie is a guy whose family, going back to his grandfather, was all cops. He's the token black sheep who never joined the force. He and his girlfriend said they wanted to perform a fantasy scene in which he would be a policeman who would arrest her for streetwalking—but then she would turn the tables on him, fucking him in the ass before they ever made it back to the precinct, taunting him for thinking he could dominate her.

On the day of the shoot, Mr. Black Sheep showed up for their scene in full uniform, with badge, nightstick, revolver, handcuffs—the whole police officer regalia. He wanted to use every bit of it as an erotic prop.

"We had no idea he was going to show up with all this stuff," Shar said. "It was incredible. There was only one thing he wouldn't do—that was when we put a donut on his girlfriend's rubber cock and asked him to eat it."

I doubled over laughing. "He'll get fucked in the ass in uniform, but he won't disrespect the donut!"

"No," Shar said, "It's better than that. He's a vegan. He won't eat donuts under any circumstances. He wouldn't budge on it"

Jack's big day started off in the morning with toast and home-made jam. In what could be only called an *unusual* situation for the porn world, he was the only man on the set—all the crew were women. This is exactly the opposite of most film sets in any genre. Jack glowed. "I love having sex while other people are doing important things around me.... It's even better when it's lesbians who all are doing very important things."

"I don't get it," I said, "is it the slacker fantasy, or what?"

"Haven't you ever been on a job, and realized that you'd rather be having sex? It can totally preoccupy you in a boring gig."

I asked Jack to tell me more details of what went on in his mind during the sex scenes.

"I liked the attention, that I was special in their eyes—but every minute that went by, I realized that what I did wasn't as much sex as it was *acting*. The timing of what they wanted on camera had nothing to do with my body's timing. Chloe would push my dick inside her and say, "Okay, we've got the IPS," (initial penetration shot), and everyone would be thrilled; then we had to go straight from that to this full-tilt fucking. There was none of the buildup you would have in real life.

"I did get soft inside her when she was humping me, because it was way too fast after I had just entered her. I was worried about what to do, but everyone said, 'That's cool, this is the acting part, we'll shoot the rest of your bodies now from the waist up.'

"Then I'd come out of her, and she would go down on me, or start to stroke me to get me hard again. I showed her how I liked her to stroke my cock, and as soon as I'd get hard again, it was time for the next position. When we were done with the script, she asked me to fist her so she could come, and that was intense—she started coming like a rocket from the moment I got my whole hand inside her."

The day after the shoot, Shar showed Jack and me an unedited clip from that very scene, with Jack literally holding little Chloe on his big hand, with her eyes rolling back in her head as she orgasms. "Can you feel it? Can you feel it?" she says to him. He flushes all over.

"Wow, that part's really hot," I said, "both of you are changing colors. This is my favorite part, and it's not even a wood section—you did real good, Jack." Donuts all around, and not a single dream deferred.

I WAS A HOLLYWOOD SEX
CONSULTANT

I'VE GIVEN A LOT OF TIPS to people about their love lives over the years—but I can't say I've ever had the chance to watch to see if they actually followed my instructions to die letter.

That's what I found so satisfying about getting a job as a cinematic sex consultant. For once, I got to ensure that all those techniques I raved about, my emphasis on the perfect caress, were played out to my most exacting standards. Yeah, it was sweet all right—I don't think I'll ever be satisfied again with handing out free (not to mention unverified) bedroom advice.

I was the "technical consultant" to a movie that soaked many a critic's wet test: *Bound,* starring Gina Gershon and Jennifer Tilly. It was the first-time feature from *Matrix* writers/directors Larry and Andy Wachowski, a film noir thriller about a pair of lesbian lovers who dare to double-cross the mob.

What was so "technical" about this film? There's quite a bit of suspense and graphic violence—and I'm the kind of girl who can't even handle the buildup of a surprise birthday cake. No, my expertise was on the characters of the butch/femme heroines, Corky (a James Dean look-alike recently paroled) and luscious Violet (a curvy mobster mistress), and how they become lovers in the first place.

It all started two years ago with a modest little fan letter, before the picture's release I got a package from Larry and Andy, attached to a script, saying that they loved my writing. They held my early bible on dykesex, *Susie Sexpert's Lesbian Sex World,* in high esteem. They said they would be honored if I would consider making a cameo appearance in their new film.

"That's nice," I thought—and not to sound spoiled, but this invitation didn't electrify me. It seems everybody is making their own movie today—including myself, since I have fashioned many an amateur production with untrained enthusiasm. I frequently get asked to pull my dress up over my head on camera, or to write dialog for some experimental video poem. I got invited to lend out my thigh-high leather boots for a colleague's dominatrix documentary. While I have applauded all my friends' virtuosity, working on their movies was a grind, and I was becoming more discriminating all the time.

Here's what was intriguing about Andy and Larry's letter: the letterhead didn't sport their names. Instead, it was embossed: "Dino De Laurentiis Studios. "Quite a calling card. DeLaurentiis is a major Hollywood producer, the man behind *Dune.* I decided to postpone loading the dishwasher, and I sat down with the script.

I didn't budge for the next hour except to scream between pages. It was one diabolical setup. The action was razor tight; the characters were whispering in my ears. This was fantastic writing. There was only one thing missing.

I wrote back to Mr. and Mr. Wachowski:

"Your script is outstanding. I'd be delighted to play your bar girl cameo. But if you don't think I'm too presumptuous, could I be your lesbian-sex consultant? I notice that whenever the two lovers fall into an embrace, it doesn't say exactly what happens next. On behalf of every moviegoer who can't live through another cornball lesbian love scene, could I please—*please*—give you my words of advice on what two women like this would do in bed together?"

They said yes. They may have even said, "Yahoo!" I met Larry and his wife, Thea, at a Holiday Inn a few weeks later, and they were the opposite of every Hollywood bullshit artist I'd encountered in the past. They weren't kidding about knowing my stuff. They could quote my own prose right back to my face. I knew they saw the dykes in their movie as having the kind of sassy, let's-get-down-to-it sensibility that I've always written about.

I don't know how many of you have seen the catalog of lesbian films over the years. Most of them, like *Personal Best* or *Desert Hearts,* concern a tender coming-out story—shyly romantic, erotically timid. I'm known to be shy and sentimental myself, but lesbian life does not begin and end with baby powder.

When you think about it, most people's best sexual experiences don't occur their first time between the sheets. As you gain more experience about who you are and what you like, your sex life improves drastically. So why are Hollywood lesbians always portrayed in the diaper stage? I longed for characters who knew what they wanted and were hungry for more. I wanted to get beyond dewy girlishness and into some pussy power.

First, I sent Larry and Andy a portrait photo from the cover of the book about lesbian erotic photography I was working on, *Nothing But the Girl.* When I first met Gina Gershon I carried the same picture in my hand: a beautiful butch woman sitting like Rodin's *Thinker,* tattooed and muscled, with a cowlick like Elvis's, but with all the shadows and soft curves of a woman's figure. The model's name was Ronny, but when I sent the picture to the Wachowskis, I wrote, "This is your Corky."

Corky's character is a revelation in Hollywood cinema, because it is the first time since the days of Marlene Dietrich and Greta Garbo that female masculinity has been eroticized. Traditionally, when we see a woman in the movies who's a "dyke," she's a mannish woman—but more than that, she's a psychopath, the social misfit. She's the prison warden, the weird jock, the brutal nurse, the fucked-up punk. When have we ever seen a gorgeous woman of our generation on-screen who moved like Jimmy Dean, sulked like a young Brando, and drew a bead on you like the Sundance Kid? Corky had to be the kind of woman whom everyone in the theater would be dying to go to bed with, and she had to do it without acting the least bit like a girly-girl.

Violet, on the other hand, couldn't be just any straight girl on the drift. She had to be a femme diva, as calculating and sensual as a cat. She's a woman who's lost a bit of her soul fucking men for money, but she knows exactly what kind of touch she needs to find redemption. Most of all—and this was the part that cracked the cliché about dangerous femme fatales—she had to be a femme you could count on, whether it was getting you off or getting you out of a jam.

The Wachowskis had the character and dialog ready to roll in their script; it was just a matter of how to keep that same feeling going in the sex scenes. Given the infantile nature of American censorship, how much could we show on-screen before we got our hand slapped by the producers? It was a frightening prospect.

I sent the brothers a couple of X-rated film clips of lesbian sex that I turned to for inspiration. One was a shower scene from Robert McCallum's *3AM,* a golden oldie of the porn world that makes every audience who's ever seen it dead silent with awe. The other piece I told them about was an art-world video I'd acted in for a friend, called *Kathy,* by Cecilia Dougherty. I loved the sex scenes in these movies, and I had some ideas about how to shoot the same sort of thing for an R rating.

There were two main ideas on my mind. One, unlike most Hollywood lesbian scenarios, this movie shouldn't insinuate oral sex—those weren't the kind of characters we were looking at. *Bound's* premise is about getting inside someone very fast, trusting them with everything. These women had to be inside each other, fucking each other. Penetration was the act we wanted to imply. Obviously we weren't going to get away with gynecological or hard-core shots in a movie that was headed for America's shopping malls. But I knew all we had to show were the right clues.

There are thousands of Hollywood heterosexual movies where we easily imagine the male and female lovers having intercourse—everything *From Here to Eternity to Basic Instinct.* So how do you imply lesbians having "intercourse"?

One of my ideas, inspired from the *Kathy* footage, was to show a woman's legs, straining and squeezing with her lover's forearm between her thighs. We dwell on that arm for a moment, moving back and forth in a fucking rhythm, unrelenting. Then, instead of following her arm all the way up to her lover's pussy, we would cut to her stomach, fluttering like a little butterfly in that spasm we all recognize as orgasm. I loved the idea of eroticizing a woman's belly like that. A lot of traditional erotic movies try to show a woman's sexual pleasure by focusing the lens on her cleavage. Maybe that's what the director was looking at, but that's not where she's coming!

The other key idea I offered was to eroticize the women's hands whenever they were flirting or making love with each other. "A lesbian's hands are her cock," I said, like some veteran pornographer. "They're the hard-on of the movie—that's what you want to follow."

When I saw Corky's hands on-screen, I wanted to imagine how they would feel inside me. Her loving hands are the metaphorical substitute for the genital shots that we wouldn't be showing.

Mommy's Little Girl

I went through my whole little consulting session alternating between glee and dread. I had gasped my way through one big-budget film consulting experience before, and it burned me like a marshmallow on a stick. In the late eighties, I was approached by a dapper man from southern California who asked me if I thought that there was a film market for a woman's erotic point of view.

Uh, yeah, as I matter of fact I did. I wouldn't even have a career if it wasn't for all die incredible women who've come out of the woodwork to write their own erotic stories, and to make their own movies, sex toys, and social lives that incorporate their genuine desires. I don't *know* a single woman who isn't disappointed with the way female sexuality is portrayed in television, women's magazines, and studio movies. It's garbage and it's insulting.

So I ended up writing the dialog for a script, called *Erotique,* with a woman director I admired, Lizzie Borden, and I loved working with the actors during that shoot. But once I was off the scene, the producer took the movie and got rid of every element that made him personally uncomfortable—and there went the movie's promise. I introduced the film during its premiere at a Seattle film fest, and had to face an angry audience who felt as if I'd personally let them down. If this was women's erotica, then it was a major sellout. I wanted to wear one of those buttons that say, I just work here." I agreed with everyone's criticism. Why no male nudity? Why all the coy lesbian pattycake and the avoidance of any man-to-man eroticism, when it was clearly in the script's intentions? Why all the gender clichés?

Up until that point I had the Good Coozie-Keeping Seal of Integrity on all my writings and projects. The moment I had signed up with this conventional Hollywood studio, my reputation was trashed. What a nightmare.

This time, I felt as if Larry, Andy, and I were on the same wavelength, but I wasn't going to be around when their producers, bean counters, and lawyers got their hands on it. This movie was going to be seen by every lesbian and lesbian lover I knew, and they would crucify me if it was anything less than authentic. I couldn't cross my fingers hard enough.

Most fans I meet ask me about the actresses in this story, rather than the directors. Before this experience, I think I'd have done the same. When you see someone on-screen blowing your mind, thrilling you with their charisma, you feel as though all your thanks and identification should rest at their feet.

Andy and Larry sure don't look like a couple of glamorous dykes, but believe me, the characters you saw up there come straight from their groovy imaginations and fertile libidos— with a little inspiration from me, their wives, and probably a lot of other artists and lovers they've admired over the years. Their actresses mirrored them, not the other way around.

I was apprehensive to meet Gina Gershon. Her role, Corky, was the one I was worried about. Every actress is trained to play a whore/mistress/siren, the physical outline of Violet's femme character. But what women in Hollywood get asked to play a sexy butch, a bulldagger you'd like to get to know inside and out?

Gina came up to meet me in San Francisco before the shoot started. It was a relief to see her in person from the moment she walked up and grabbed my hand. She was physically right for the part: dark and handsome and brooding, no problem.

I blurted out, "I hope you don't think this is some granola-chewing, Birkenstock-wearing lesbo girl on the page here"— and she laughed out loud. Gina was already on the right track, thinking about the most erotically compelling male icons in movie history to draw her machisma from. She wasn't a dyke in her personal life, but she had been around the block. That's what I wanted. It wouldn't have done anybody a favor to have a genuine panty-tested lesbian if she had been a Pollyanna or a prude. Most important, Gina was an experienced actor. I gave her some books, and directions to the sleaziest, sweatiest lesbian club night I could think of. She was set.

My last gift to cinematic realism was just before my trip down to L.A. to shoot my cameo scene. I was to play my cameo as a fetching babe in a dive that Corky tries unsuccessfully to pick up. My big line is "Hello," but I look like a fox.

I knew the bar scene would be stocked with extras to make it look like a happening place. If the studio was sending over actors from a typical Hollywood casting agency—I shuddered.

Please don't let them send in the clowns. Los Angeles is such a closeted town. Women are so uptight about their femininity there; it's the plastic surgery and dieting capital of the world. It would be hard to find extras who looked like liberated dykes. I called Larry again and asked if they could find it within their budget to let me bring down a handful of authentic babes from San Francisco who would make our set really look like a lesbian joint, instead of a juice bar. They said yes—thank you, Daddy! We spent all day shooting that barroom scene, but it looked just right in the final cut.

The first time I saw *Bound* was in front of fifteen hundred delirious women and a couple hundred very curious men. I arranged for the San Francisco Gay and Lesbian Film Festival to host the premiere of the movie in the Castro Theater: a grandiose art-deco movie house that still has an organist rising out of the pit pounding the keys with "San Francisco, Open your Golden

Gates." You feel like putting on your opera gloves and raising a glass of champagne before you enter the theater.

Larry, Andy, their wives Thea and Alise, assistant Phil, Gina, the film's editor, and our illustrious extras arrived at the entrance in a white limousine. I was squeezing Larry's and Andy's palms so tight they're lucky they can still hold a pen. Everyone in the house had heard that I was the "sex consultant." I think they imagined that meant I stood over Gina and Jennifer with a riding crop, snapping, "Deeper, harder, a little to the left!"

The festival director introduced our small mob onto the stage, and I put on my most radiant smile. Some idiot from the festival's sponsoring advertisers got up to the mike to plug why "Everyone should buy an Isuzu SUV." He was filled with all that new gay marketing rhetoric, and he told the packed house with utter seriousness that the new Isuzu was the top choice among today's lesbian automobile shoppers.

Such tackiness could drive me out of my mind before our beautiful film's debut. As soon as the man walked off the stage, I grabbed the mike, and said, "I don't know about you, but most lesbians I know are still taking the bus." The crowd went crazy (was that our first standing ovation?)—and after that every single moment was like a dream come true.

The movie looked like butter. The actors were on fire, the audience picked up every erotic cue and innuendo, and they screamed just like I had a year ago in my kitchen, turning the pages. When the end came, they exploded in an orgy of gratitude. I thought we were going to be carried out on the crowd's shoulders.

Larry and Andy said they'd made up their minds never to watch the movie again after that Castro premiere, and they've stuck to their decision. They said it couldn't get any better, so let it be the finest and last memory of the audience who completely and utterly "got it."

I'm more of a glutton, I'm afraid. When the movie finally opened in my hometown, I took nine different field trips with my friends. I watched it with my dad; I watched it with my daughter's first-grade teacher and her husband; I watched it with my ex-girlfriends, who I must say, provided as much of my consulting wisdom as anyone else you could mention.

I'm just so filled with gay-fucking-pride, I'm ready to burst. But here's the thing, see, I'm bisexual—and I think those romantic scenes in Hollywood boy-girl epics are awfully tired. *Snore.* Give me a call, boys. I know there are a thousand directors with a healthy budget in Hollywood right now, ready to shoot their much-anticipated sex scene and dreading every moment of it. I'll make you feel a whole lot better, Mr. Director. This will be the part of your movie that folks will talk about forever. You don't even have to give me a cameo. Just let me get my hands on the words.

CHECKING OUT

I RECEIVED SALLY BINFORD'S good-bye letter the day after her body was found.

To those I love—

Most of you know that for some time I've been planning to check out—not out of despair or depression, but a desire to end things well. I've been lucky enough to have had a remarkable life immeasurably enriched by the love and support of a large (if improbable) group of friends and lovers. I don't want to let it fizzle out in years of debility and dependency. I've gambled enough to know that quitting while you're ahead (or at least even) is wise.

And those of you familiar with my birthday will recognize that the timing of my exit allows me to claim as my epitaph:

Toujours soixante-neuf!

Love and good-bye,

Sally

Sally had planned for many years to "check out" before her seventieth birthday, but I always thought it was a vague promise, along the lines of "gonna die before I get old." Sally was more youthful in spirit than me, and I was half her age, so I figured I'd never see that day.

But I did see the day, in the form of a phone call from my ex, Honey, telling me that Sally had really gone and done it. She had cleaned her house, put all her affairs in order, and given herself and her beloved poodle, Jake, a perfect good-bye cocktail of narcotics. She died peacefully, and exactly as she had designed.

I cried like a baby on the phone, "I just saw her a couple days ago, and she said *nothing* to me, nothing." Honey told me that Sally had sent out letters. The next day, there mine was, lying on the floor under the mail slot. No return address. It looked from the envelope like a party invitation, or some subversive plot she was hatching. It was, indeed, the most subversive scheme she'd ever designed.

I opened the envelope and found a typewritten note Sally had photocopied for her longtime friends, lovers, and those family members with whom she was still on speaking terms. In the letter, she sounded just as confident, determined, and funny as ever. *"Toujours Soixante-Neuf!"* she proclaimed at the end. That was her motto: "Forever sixty-nine!"

Sally Binford, as anyone who knew her will tell you, was an astonishing person. A pioneering anthropologist and archeologist, her writings on prehistory are required reading for most college courses in those disciplines. A passionate antiwar activist who dropped out of academia at the height of her career in the 1960s, she was one of the founding mothers of the modem feminist movement, a charter member of NOW. But beyond that, she was the first woman ever (if you don't count Emma Goldman) who I'd call the very model of a sex-positive feminist.

Sally was the living embodiment of radical sexual liberation— free from the bonds of jealousy, monogamy, and any and all love arrangements based on the idea of private property. She was one of the members of Sandstone, the infamous Malibu center for communal free love and rigorous chess playing. She was the female "star" of the only movie ever made about the sex lives of old people, *A Ripple in Time,* which she made with her dear friend Ed Brecher when she was in her late 50s. Sally was a one-of-a-kind sex educator and a trailblazer to the very end, the only bisexual member of the very first Old Lesbian Conference steering committee. Sometimes she'd end a phone call with me, saying she had to go to a Gray Panthers meeting and I'd wonder how the rest of them could possibly keep up with her.

Ms. Binford could convert anyone to the cause of erotic cama-raderie and social insurrection. She was so smart, so witty, an intellectual's delight, a revolutionary's inspiration, and above all, a hell of a lot of fun. She made her homes in Maui, San Francisco, and southern France, near the caves at Lascaux. Her poker parties, which brought some of the finest minds in town to the table, were notorious. Her Thanksgiving and Christmas suppers were legendary. She loved me to pieces, and I guess that's the thing that gets to me the most.

Forget famous Sally, or notorious Sally, and you'd still find someone who would do anything for the people she loved—except live past her prime.

A year after Sally's death—and months after everyone who'd ever loved her had met at the enormous wake she requested—her longtime lover and companion Jeremy Slate wrote to each of us, asking what we made of Sally's choice to die. He wrote:

I believe in her dying, Sally had something to say, a point to make. Not unlike her, hey?

To clarify that point, to continue to reap the rewards of having known Sally, we should examine our feelings and let them be known to each of us.

If you agree please answer a couple of questions and add some of your own:

Were you aware that Sally was planning to die when she was still sixty-nine? How'd you find out?

What was your emotional response/reaction upon learning of her death?

Where did your reasoning take you? What, ultimately, did you think of Sally's choice?

What are your feelings now, nearly two months later?

Love,

Jeremy

I wrote Jeremy a long reply, filled with all my mixed-up feelings. Yes, Sally had told me about her plan to "check out" according to her own design, and I hadn't liked it, although I wouldn't dream of trying to talk her out of it. She was the first person to ever prompt me to consider what I'm am going to do when my life is at its end.

Was I aware that Sally was planning to die when she was still 69?

Sally first told me about her plans to check out more than a year ago on a car trip we took to M. and R.'s ranch. We were on the winding forest road that leads to their place when she brought it up. She was sixty-eight at the time. She told me she had no intention of living past sixty-nine blah blah, her usual rap about how she'd planned this for a long time. By way of explanation, she added that her whole family tended to fall apart after seventy years of age.

She spoke of three people who were influential in her wishes. First, there was Ed Brecher (a fellow sex researcher and educator), who had taken his life a year earlier, also according to plan. She felt comradeship with Ed in their mutual decision to check out when old age became intolerable. Then there was her friend Jeanette, who she thought was the most awful example of someone brilliant and vital who'd turned into a virtual idiot and invalid before Sally's very eyes.

Finally, she brought up Honey Lee—my ex-lover and the person who brought Sally and I together ten years ago. She said that Honey Lee opposed her plans and was not supportive. She got so angry just thinking about it!

She brought up Honey's opinions as if to ask, "Do you agree with her?" Sally always treated us like a couple which considering the way I still relate to HL, was not that far from the truth.

124

I remember protesting, "Sally, it's not that Honey Lee doesn't support your decision, it's just that she doesn't want to do that damn plastic bag thing!"

That was true. The very first time I heard about Sally's suicide plan was when Honey Lee and I lived together, in the mideighties, and Honey Lee told me that Sally wanted to enlist her help. The critical question was whether Honey Lee would have the wherewithal to wrap a plastic bag over Sally's head and finish her off should the dose of sleeping pills fail. This, Honey Lee could not see herself doing.

I could just imagine Sally's matter-of-fact discussion of plastic bag asphyxiation techniques while Honey looked on in horror. Honey Lee can't even put a live lobster in a pot of boiling water. I was surprised that Sally couldn't see that no matter how much someone loves you, they don't necessarily have the temperament to help you kill yourself!

I told Sally that it was easy for me to support her decision to die when she wanted to, that I had thought of doing die same thing myself when the time came. But it seemed so abstract to me then, like something I could only consider when I was a great deal older. Sally had made up her mind before she was fifty.

I knew I didn't have any moral dilemmas about taking my life. It makes me angry when people get outraged or punitive about suicide. It's the people who are alive who suffer, really. The dearly departed are no longer feeling anything at all—happiness or pain. I'm not the type who relishes death or thinks about suicide in earnest, but I never thought it was wrong.

I did tell Sally—and this is where I cried a little—that I would miss her so much and that I couldn't stand to think about not having her near me She was very loving to me when I said that; she kissed me and patted my knee as she was driving. She seemed relieved that I didn't oppose her plan. Honestly, our main argument seemed to be which one of us understood Honey Lee's feelings correctly!

Sally only made occasional, lighthearted references to checking-out after that afternoon. What's interesting to me now, in retrospect, is that I never mentioned it again, ever, as if by my not speaking of it, I could somehow postpone the event. When she passed her sixty-ninth birthday without incident, I was so relieved. I figured she had changed her mind and decided to live on until she was genuinely disabled. I never compared or shared my explanation with her, because I was afraid, I guess. I was avoiding the truth.

Sally didn't involve me in her death plans except to make very sure that she saw me a couple of days before she died. We had a wonderful time. She met my current lover, whom she obviously approved of and enjoyed, and I met her old friend Sarah and partner Don. We all got on really well. I remember feeling like a party pooper because when I announced it was time to go home and relieve my baby-sitter, it was clear we could have all rolled off the dinner table and gone to bed together in a minute She did kiss me on the mouth before I went out the door, but that seemed like just her usual affection for me—not any big poignant good-bye.

During that last dinner, we had Sally's usual feast: French country cooking, a new Beaujolais. We drank Armagnac after the plates were cleared, with Sally's hand-rolled Three Castles tobacco, Maui sinsemilla, and pretty little lines of cocaine laid out on her pocket mirror. It was so luxurious, and she made it look so easy. I thought for the hundredth time, "Sally is a total cokehead. This can't be good for her"—and once more I kicked myself: "You know perfectly well Sally is going to check out, so she might as well do whatever she pleases."

What was my emotional response/reaction upon learning of her death?

I was at my lover Ion's house fooling around in the garden with my three-year-old daughter Aretha. Jon, a painter, was gessoing a canvas. The phone rang Jon answered it, then came over to me with his face all screwed up and said, "Honey Lee has to talk to you, Susie; it's terrible news."

I assumed something had happened to Honey. Interestingly, I thought she had been diagnosed with cancer, suspecting that her daily pack of Shermans had finally done her in. I got cold all over.

Honey was crying. She said, "Sally's dead."

I folded over like I'd been hit on the head, and water gushed out of my body hot sweat from my pores and tears from my eyes like a flood. I was so overcome it made Honey stop weeping, and she told me she had just gotten the news from Jeremy.

What was unexpected was my daughter's reaction. She came to me while I was crying on the phone and hugged my leg. She looked so worried. Jon and I told her that Sally was my friend, and I loved her, but that she had died and it made me so sad.

Aretha remembers this moment, and brings up Sally's death to this day. One night, months after Sally's death, I gave her a notepad and a pen to doodle with in the car while we were driving home from school.

"This is Sally dying," she said, right out of the blue, holding up the notepad after she'd been drawing for a while. I asked her a bit more about it

Mommy's Little Girl

Aretha said that "Sally is sad," and "she has on a shirt and she has on pants and she's turning round and round until she dies."

I said, "Well, I was sad when Sally died, but I think Sally was happy. She had a really big life and she was ready to go."

For years after Sally's death, when Aretha saw me sad or crying, she always asked about Sally, and whenever we talked about something being dead, even a leaf on the ground, she would say, "like Sally."

I never experienced the death of anyone dose to me when I was young. Sally is the first intimate friend of mine to die I've had other friends and family who died after I had been apart from them for a long time like my grandparents. Although it was tragic, I felt at a great distance from the loss.

"This is Sally dying."

Mommy's Little Girl

What do I think of Sally's choice?

The one thing I can't figure out, the one thing I wish I had asked her, is how she could resist living when she was in such excellent mental and physical shape? Sally was an athlete, she had a beautiful body, everything worked, she could party us all under the table and get up at six the next morning to walk with her dog.

I certainly have had an interesting life, a full life, but even after my daughter is grown, or I've seen more of the world, it will be so hard for me to think, "There. I've done it. I've done enough." What if there were something more?

The closest I came to being mad at her was thinking, "Oh, she just had to stick to her little plan. Little Miss Control can't stand to change her mind—once it's on the calendar, that's it."

I also realize now how very secretive Sally was about certain things. That's ironic because her politics and philosophy were all about honesty and openness. She had to pull off a great performance hiding the things she did. I don't understand that part of her. Of course we all have secrets, we all put people on, but our styles of discretion and privacy were different. I don't know why she kept certain things from me and her other loved ones.

I also wonder, as a mother, how she felt about dying before Susan, her adult daughter who's ill with multiple sclerosis. It's always been difficult for me to understand why the two of them had such a hard time with each other—another secret.

Of course, I understand mothers and daughters feuding. But while I confided in Sally a lot about the distress between my own mother and I, she never did the same with me.

She did talk a lot about Susan's illness, her grandchildren, and son-in-law—who she always referred to as a "saint." Susan was obviously on her mind a lot and she often spoke of her daughter's animosity toward her; how it developed when Susan was a teenager. But she treated it like an act of fate; something there was no rational explanation for. I know Sally could be annoyingly rational and stubborn, but she was so caring to me that I felt I received a mother's unconditional love from her.

I also wish I could have asked Sally about how her view of romantic love changed, because after all, she was married three times and wasn't always a bisexual polyamorist. There were more secrets: she never told me why she married any of those men, or confessed to any sentimental or romantic feelings she might have had about old or current lovers. She respected her third husband and research partner in academia, Lou Binford, for his mind and ambition, but that was it.

When I was once terribly in love—in an affair with "Bad News" written all over it—Sally was very sympathetic about the self-destructive aspect of it, my desire to live on hot coals. She said she had done that in the past, too. But I couldn't possibly imagine her in my situation! I never saw her bent out of shape over love.

I remember when she and G. were breaking up. She was really mad, but she was so typically cut-and-dried about it. "Thank God I've got my house back to myself again," she said. And then she seemed to be good friends with G. almost immediately, without ever expressing loss or grief—she was just a little pissed.

I guess I didn't ask Sally these questions because I would get caught up in her charismatic common sense. I didn't want to be girly and silly either, let alone pry into her past for some tender or painful revelations.

Mommy's Little Girl

What are my feelings now?

I have had a lot of dreams about Sally visiting me, unexpectedly. I say she's "haunting" me. In one dream, I am involved in some very stressful, chaotic situation, when all of a sudden Sally comes around the corner like the Cheshire Cat. "What are you doing here, you're supposed to be dead!" I say. She tells me that it was all a big trick, that she's not really dead, but that now I'm the only one who can see her. I feel like Cosmo in the <u>Topper</u> movies. I get so mad at her, shouting, "How could you upset everyone like this, just as a ruse?" and I tell her that I can't shoulder the burden of being the only one who can see her.

The night before we held Sally's wake, I dreamed a slightly different scenario. Once again, she popped up in the middle of total chaos, but instead of being mad at her, I was relieved and I ran into her arms. I told her I was going to her wake, that nothing was going to stop me, and she was so happy to hear it.

Then she kissed me on the mouth—it was so vivid. I could feel the dry wrinkles of her lips pressing against my own. It was like a sex dream that instantly wakes you up.

I remember the sunset the evening after Sally died. I was alone in my room looking out the window at the ocean, and it was pink and red and blue. I've never done this before, but I stuck my head out the window and talked to the sunset as if it were Sally.

We don't often have spectacular sunsets in San Francisco; it's so overcast. When I see one now, at Ocean Beach, Sally's sky comes back to my mind. I can see it exactly, every color.

I realize, inasmuch as Sally wrote me a letter I could not reply to, I have responded nevertheless, with a story that I can only release into the air, and into anyone's hands that it falls upon.

my so-called
sex life

THE BEST SHE EVER HAD

I PRESSED JON TO TELL ME more about Carrie. The wind was carrying voices from the cafe brunchers onto our beach spot, but I pulled another towel over my head and heard only him.

"She said a lot of nice things about me—she's so complimentary."

"Like what?" I imagined what she might say— "Sir, you have a very nice cock." That's what I would say to Jon if I'd just had a one-night stand with him: "Nice cock, beautiful hair."

"She said... okay, this is embarrassing she said, I was the best lover she'd ever had!"

"You're kidding!"

"Yeah, incredible as it may seem..."

"You know I don't mean—"

We both buried our heads in the beach towel and laughed.

"Yeah, I know what *you* mean," he said, and nudged my crotch with his toe.

I sat up in the sand so I could see him better. We were both struggling with our straw hats in the wind.

I decided to speculate. "Maybe what Sheila said about her being so sexually inexperienced is true."

"But she's thirty-two!"

"Thirty-two-year-old sex today is what sixteen-year-old sex was in our day—just creeping out of the egg."

"Is it really that bad?"

"Yeah, well think about it—if she was holding out through high school, and then 'playing it safe' in college, that doesn't leave a lot of time for sodomy and wasted nights."

"That's such a shame... but then what about all those blow jobs she talked about? It fits in, though, doesn't it? She's afraid of everything else."

Tell me that part again, about her first boyfriend." I dug my toes into the sand until they hit the wet part.

"She said she just broke up with her first real boyfriend, and that when they got together, she promised him a thousand blow jobs. She got up to seven hundred and forty-nine in three years."

"Seven hundred and forty-nine!"

"Yes!"

"Now, that seems like a magic number. I'll never forget it, and I've only heard it once. But I don't see how she managed to keep track... I mean, I tried to do that, when I was first fucking, but every time I went to bed with someone new, I'd change my idea about what good sex was, or what love was, and then my old system didn't make any sense."

"Well, maybe it's easier with blow jobs, if that's all you're doing."

"But she didn't come, going down on you, did she?"

"No, of course not! It was hard for her to come; she kept trying to block me. She couldn't believe I wouldn't try to fuck her, trick her—and then when I went down on her, she didn't think I really wanted to eat her. She kept not believing, and not believing, and all that made her orgasm remote."

"I bet the women who actually orgasm giving head don't count the number... If you want to swallow cock all the time, if that gets you off, you aren't competitive about it; you're just hungry, right? I mean, who keeps track of how many times they eat their favorite meal?"

Jon dropped his voice. "She was kind of rare, you know; she swallowed everything, every drop."

"Oh Jon, oh God—that makes me feel like such an asshole—Jon, that's not so rare, I've just brainwashed you. I'm terrible."

"Is that so? You're the only one who's not swallowing? You should repent, then."

"I can't; it's too late. You know I don't give a shit about blow-jobs. But don't you remember, when we were first together, I did the whole deep-throat number. That's part of the BJ-macha thing, to show a guy what you're made of."

"I don't remember any of that!"

"See? I told you I was mediocre at it. Well, I didn't do it for that long, 'cause we got so comfortable and if you *really* only wanted blow jobs from me, the whole thing would have fallen apart after two dates."

"What *did* I want from you?" Jon turned around and started tracing a circle in the small of my back.

"You wanted me to be a good girl and come really hard for you!"

"You're such a good girl, then—"

"And you like to show me, don't you?"

"Is *that* rare?"

"No! No! It's not. It's what practically everyone feels, and if they weren't so insecure and doing their stupid little dance maneuvers, everybody would just take it for granted." I pulled off my sunhat and ducked my head against his chest. I didn't know if he could hear me talking into his heart. "When you fuck me, you *know* I feel it, and I know you feel me giving it up to you. And that's what it's all about; it's not so complicated!"

He lifted my head up. "Do you want to stamp your foot now?"

"I'm going to stamp it real hard!"

"You don't have to get mad at Carrie—"

"I'm not, I'm practically praying for her, it's just the whole thing that makes me mad—all these BJ queens who can't come, won't come One day they'll wanna have a baby, and after that, all their competition and affection will go to their children and they'll never wanna have sex again. I think the blow-job queen of today is the celibate of tomorrow. You better teach Carrie something about her sexual self-interest before it's too late" '

"You could teach her, too—"

"She's not attracted to me!"

"You don't know that—"

"Oh c'mon! Yes I do. She's not the least bit queer. And if she ever does anything with a girl, it's going to be with another little flower like herself, not some predatory old bag."

Jon leaned over and bit my ass cheek.

"Ouch! Fuck you! You know what I'm talking about. I am not convincing some squeamish straight girl into accepting my ministrations. Talk about humiliation."

"You're making an awful lot of assumptions."

"Yeah, well, tell her I want the, uh, two hundred . . . and fifty-one blow jobs she forgot to give her ex. I'll strap on my biggest tool."

"But I wanna do that part."

"You're a greedy little pig. What I wanna know is, when are you going to see her next?"

"I don't know; I can't see her this week, and she can't see me next week, and I don't even know what week it is after that, but she really wants to get together."

"That's so crippled! When I found anyone who qualified as the "best lover I ever had,' I was driving all night to see them after a twelve-hour shift; I was hitching rides, telling lies, Jesus Christ! If she's telling the truth, you're in for it."

"That's right, you used to drive to Nevada from San Francisco to see me."

"Every week, then every three days—"

"Every day you weren't working."

"Well, that's what I mean, why can't she just come up and see you for one fucking night? She only lives an hour away, and you're the one who has a kid and a day job. Is she afraid of seeing me, of being in our house?"

"That's probably part of it."

"Have you told her we have separate bedrooms, the life of polyamorous luxury?"

"I told her we have plenty of room, and that she could spend the night, but I just think this openness is sort of new to her. She asked what it would be like with you here."

"And what did you say?"

"I said she might get devoured like a little bunny."

"Oh my God, did that make her scream?"

"Yes!"

"You shouldn't do that—"

"But it's her not-so-secret secret fear!"

"Well, I prefer to play hard to get. I prefer to demonstrate that I don't give a shit! You should really tell her it's like having a friend over that you spend some time alone with."

"Well that *is* what it's like, exactly, but I can't just convince her of that by saying it. She has to be here for a few minutes and see for herself."

"Christ, I feel like the *Addams Family* sometimes... 'Good evening, we're nonmonogamous... Can Pugsly get you a drink?'"

I pushed my glasses up my nose, they kept slipping. "I'm getting burnt; we have to find some shade."

"You can have my shirt."

"Baby..."

Jon covered me in a white surfer competition T-shirt that said *"Stand Tall, Be Proud."*

"I'm embarrassed to be seen with this kind of propaganda on my chest. I wanna replace this slogan with something like *'Lay Down, Seek Humility.'*"

"How about *'Lay Down, Deliver 749 Blow Jobs'*?"

"I can't get over what a magic number that is! It's because it ends in nine, I think; it sounds like something unfinished." I pulled the sweatshirt hood over my face.

"Maybe seven hundred and forty-nine is just approximate."

"I don't think so, I think she has a feeling for numbers and for signs. And when she has more sexual experiences, she'll still have an intuition about the cycles of things, the beauty of repetition—Jon, when you were in your twenties, who would you have said was 'the best lover you ever had'?"

"Why my twenties?"

"Because I'm not trying to be coy, and that was before I met you, and I want you to think back to that point. What would you have said?"

"The best lover... that's really hard."

I poked a hole in the sand with my finger until I hit a piece of glass. It was hard to think about. I flipped through my own memories like a fan of cards that I couldn't pick from.

Jon said something first. "You know, even though she was my first lover, we were in junior high, and we didn't have intercourse, Marie was really into sex, and we had a lot of sex."

"I know. I can't believe the things you guys did under the Catholic guise of protecting her virginity."

"We were so in love and it was so intense I didn't even go out with another girl for the rest of high school after she dumped me."

"You know what?" I held up the fragment of green glass like a piece of evidence. "I think that when you're young, the first time you have sex when it doesn't hurt, and you actually come—which is more of a girl thing, I know—and there isn't some awful black cloud hanging over you—that sex automatically becomes 'the best sex,'—'the best lover' you ever had. The fact that it's even reasonably good sex is incredible when you've never known those feelings before When you get older—especially as you get older—the memory just gets more golden."

"That's what I'm saying, that even though I had a lot of deep experiences, and more variety, later—"

"Yes, it's not the same then, you're not thinking, 'Oh this is the best,' because you're in the moment, and it's unique and it doesn't seem fair to make comparisons anymore. I remember when I first had two boyfriends, and they both blew my mind, and I felt so guilty at the time, because I couldn't decide who was the 'best.' They both really were my mentors, I couldn't give either of them up."

"Are you talking about Sam? Or Cary?"

"Both of them... I was seventeen when I met Sam. He was the one who said, 'Go ahead, play with your clit.' And of course I came really hard, and then I asked him, 'Are you mad at me?' And he laughed, like the kind of laugh with tears in your eyes, because it must have been so endearing. That was my first inkling that my lover would get off because I was hot, not because I was 'making' him hot. And he was the one who was the 'set your chickens free!' type—He would say, 'Oh, stop shaving your legs, Susie.' and sometimes he'd even get annoyed with me, like, 'Hey, you're seventeen-year-old cherrycake, everyone wants to fuck you no matter what you look like."

"He was jealous of you, then."

"You're right. He was, because he used to hustle himself, and he was so matter-of-fact about what men are looking for, and he already felt like he was past his prime Men are so much harder on other men, when it comes to sex. Like, they'd fuck any girl, but another man has to be perfect."

"Maybe all women are already perfect."

"Yeah, right, we all bathe in seven-hundred-and-forty-nine-like luminescence—but I wanna tell you about my other contender, the other man I was seeing the same time as Sam. That guy, Cary, was so different. He didn't say a lot, but he just ate me up with a look. He seemed to read my cunt, or maybe I just didn't realize that all my secrets weren't so unusual."

"What secrets?"

"You already know them, too; it's just knowing what happens when a woman gets aroused, when you can torture her . . . just starting to push your cock in, and then pulling it back, and feeling her with your fingers, how she's getting puffier and puffier."

"Like a little catcher's mitt—"

"Yeah, and then her clit head starts to disappear up her pussy lips, and the cream is just getting creamier—"

"And then you nail her."

"Finally, yeah. God, just talking about it, my cunt is spreading rings—no, no, don't check me—trust me, I wanna finish telling you this, because I'm just figuring it out now. I didn't realize that Cary learned from a lot of women, I thought it was all about me and him. Because he said so little, I thought he'd practically made up my whole orgasm by himself, whereas Sam had made me talk to him, which shamed me but kind of liberated me in the next five minutes, if you know what I mean."

"So did you ever give one of them up?"

"No, I didn't, because at that time everyone was non-monogamous, and we were all fucking other people, and we were all fomenting a revolution, and I just thought we'd always keep coming back together. When Cary didn't follow me to Pittsburgh, and Sam moved to Seattle and got on his high horse about a new girlfriend, I was really shocked. And I had such bad sex in Pittsburgh; I started to wonder if everyone was retarded east of Barstow. My heart just broke one day, and I think that was the moment—that was it—that was the first time I ever said to myself. That was the best sex I ever had.' I cried my heart out. I only said it because it was gone, it was over, and I was just left a wreck. Maybe the best lover you ever had is the first one who makes you wanna die."

"Like Marie with me." Jon looked kind of crinkly.

"Oh, baby, don't... I bet she's the one crying now."

"I wouldn't want her to cry; she's had such hard time."

"Well, now she's a born-again Christian, so she can just get down off the cross—someone else needs the wood."

"I wish you could meet her."

"I wish I could meet Sam and Cary—again. I did see Sam a few years ago, at a wedding, and it kind of freaked me out. He acted scandalized by me, like I was some kind of freak, and it took all I could to bite my tongue and not say, 'Hey Sam, do you ever miss your old days whoring on Dupont Circle?' Damn, I always figured he knew more about sex than me"

"But you grew up ..."

"Yeah—into an old bag that knows more about sex than he does!"

"Shut up."

"An old bag with juicy fruit inside?"

"Let me taste it."

"It's got sand in it now."

"You're fussy."

"You're a slut. Call Carrie; tell her time waits for no blow-job queen!"

"Are you going to be jealous, after all this?"

"Maybe I will, just for the hell of it, just to see if it still has some bite."

"Sometimes your jealousy gets you in trouble"

"That's the reckless thrill of it, but I haven't been swept out to sea yet."

"You know you are the best lover I've ever had."

The tide was coming in.

"You don't have to say that!"

"But it's true you are."

"I love you—"

"Shhh... pick up the blankets."

"I do, you're the something I'll always have, I'll always feel you inside of me like nine-million-nine-thousand-ninety-nine-nine to infinity."

We kissed with our mouths open, and the sunblock on our faces stuck together. The water came up fast and pooled up around my ankles; I couldn't see if the towels were floating away. Jon took my breast out of my shirt and sucked on my nipple like a caramel. I stared up at the sun and felt the whole bag of every-thing go pop, and disappear up, all the way up, into the sky.

BOOK-TOUR DIARY

Labor Day, Los Angeles

This is where my tour begins, on the freeways near where I grew up. I lost my virginity in Los Angeles, sexually and politically.

I last lived here in the seventies, when Hollywood was still only a colony. LA thrived on shipyards, aerospace, tourism, oil fields, education. I could hitchhike from the Sunset Strip to Topanga Canyon Beach and get a different ride every time, a new set of eyes.

Now the whole sprawl is a company town, as sure as Harlan County. If any other industries exist, it is only to feed Hollywood. A shipyard can make some real money as a location. A university is a postproduction fat farm. You can make real money in servitude to the stars.

So how is LA's love life? I went to Skylight Books in Los Feliz, and my high school Spanish teacher, Mr. Gomez, showed up for my reading. He was so handsome in his old age, with his silver hair and orange *guayabera*, but his hands were shaking. He got up and told the whole crowd that the kids like me, the ones who shut down the school when Nixon invaded Cambodia, who exposed the undercover narcs and caravanned to Wounded Knee—that it all went to shit after us.

He said the kids didn't care anymore. It seemed that he could cry easily, and he did.

I don't think most of the crowd knew that I existed in any form before my incarnation as a sexpert. They didn't know LA existed in any other form besides its illusion-factory incarnate.

They paused for Mr. Gomez—but then, in one aching unified voice, they said—"There is no love here!" Anyone can get laid, but no one can have a relationship. Everything is ephemeral; passion doesn't last.

"But that's theater," I said. "When you live in a town that's based on the values of a stage, what do you expect? I don't know how to fall in love in LA anymore, either."

The next afternoon I went to visit Paul Krassner's house in Venice, the man who edited *The Realist,* and who seems to have been at every crucial counterculture moment in history since the day he was born—the bohemian *Forrest Gump.* I put on my bathing suit and zoris to walk down the boardwalk, just like we used to, back in the day—get a slice at Wavecrest, another one for the dog.

But no one just wears their swimsuit or trunks on the boardwalk any longer. I walked past a thousand people on the boardwalk, and I was the only one. The women today wear special titillating outfits that promise a lot and show rather little, at least compared to my plain bikini. You used to be able to have a fat ass and wear a string bikini and shades; you could walk down the boardwalk with a joint in your mouth and fall in love. Now it's an audition. Paul's house was filled with boxes, and he told me he was moving to the desert.

San Luis Obispo

There's one independent bookstore in town, The Phoenix.

They flourish, selling collectors' items and used books; they also offer a room that doesn't feel like a savings-and-loan office, where you can sit down and turn a page. Mostly students come to my talk, but one guy shows up who asks me how to marry a stripper. He gives me a color-photo business card advertising the gentlemen's club where he spends most of his hours... it's one block down the street. He says the girls there aren't making enough money, that someone's gotta do something. As much as he pines for them, I think this big, husky guy vicariously lives in their shadow. If he could wave a magic thong over his body and become as kittenish as "Tawny," the dancer pictured on the business card, he would.

Big Sur

I arranged a reading at the Henry Miller Library, a store/cabin set in an avant-garde sculpture garden, with a wood stove in the center of the floor and Henry's memorabilia all over the walls. I feel as if I am in the womb of the erotic intelligentsia. Every book and vintage postcard here is a template of sexual liberation—the kind that happened before the 1960s.

My audience is largely made up of folks my parents' age, some of Miller's peers. Over seventy. A local friend points out some folks who are living in a threesome today that they started decades ago. People here get to be timelessly erotic and psychedelic because the sunsets they get to watch each night cast a spell on them. It's unshakable, a timeless bohemia. I don't want to budge.

Santa Cruz

Santa Cruz is my home, and a great homecoming awaits me at the local bookshop. This reading, I realize that people my age and older are bringing their kids to see me—my first generational jump. One teenager comes up to me and says, "My mom just handed me a pile of your books when I was fifteen, and said, 'It's all here.' I told her I wasn't interested in sex— but that changed recently..." She blushes. I redden, too. A woman who used to picket me in the 1980s, for crimes against feminism, shows up at my event to announce her erotic-writing workshop.

San Francisco

I've got a noontime reading in the financial district. I want to be especially pornographic for this lunchtime event, because the nine-to-five set working downtown is so needy.

In the evening, I read at a bookshop across from City Hall, and a group of seminary students arrive. They've come to see me as a class project. They are erotic Methodists, sexually forward Presbyterians. I tell them that one of my earliest supporters was a young man whose grandfather invented Dial-a-Prayer. I suggest to them that they start a similar free hotline of erotic inspiration and meditation.

Sebastapol

Some of the world's best pornographers live here. My friends Jack Fritscher and Mark Hemry are godfathers of primal gay erotica. Jack was the first to publish Mapplethorpe's erotic photography, and he was the original editor of *Drummer*. He's like an erotic Waldo, appearing at every important moment in queer history. Their home is like a splendid gallery.

Among other things, they create fetish videos. Mark jokes to me that their big problem at the moment is that frustrated fans are demanding to see movies of men smoking a pipe nude. The special skill of "pulling on one's pipe" is what's called for here, and I'm not making a pun. Apparently there aren't enough good-looking young men around who know how to smoke a pipe properly anymore, with the right flair.

"I don't know how to smoke a pipe, but I'd slay 'em with a bong," I say. "You know, the seventies nostalgia binge is exploding now. You should send out a questionnaire asking how many of them want to see naked bong hits."

Arcata

I'm invited to speak at the local college in an "Intro to Human Sexuality" class. I give the students a little anonymous sex survey:

Do they masturbate?

Have they had sex with another person?

Do they like their sex life as it is?

Of course they're curious; no one ever talks about these sorts of things in class.

I'm surprised at how many of them are already married—they're all under twenty-four. Getting married young is popular again; it's a romantic backlash against AIDS and against the spectacle of their divorced and jaded parents. They're living the dream of a straight-edge promise, a monogamous love that never dies; even though I think they're in for a big surprise, I can't help but be touched by their sincerity.

One twenty-two-year-old husband comes up to me with his wife after class, and asks me how he can please her more. He says he loves her so much; he'd do anything and she blushes when he says that. It's those high pink cheeks again, the holy sacrament of my tour.

"Aw, you could read a million books," I say. "But when you love each other like this, if you'll do anything you hardly need instructions, you just need time."

I ask the young woman if she ever comes on her own, if she could bring herself to orgasm.

She looked down at the floor. "Well, not with my hands, but with water. You know, in the bathtub." She exhaled as if she'd laid something very heavy on the school desk. They were both so still that I felt like I'd hypnotized them, that they had to tell me the truth no matter what I asked.

"Oh, then you two have to have a bathtub party, where he gets in first and cradles you and touches you while you spray the water down on your clit."

God, it's great to give instructions like this to newlyweds. They thanked me and said goodbye, leaving a couple books behind on a seat.

Eugene, Oregon

I barely made it to the women's bookstore in town; it was such a long drive from California. The bookshop owners stalled for time by telling the crowd how independent bookstores are getting the screws put to them by the mainstream publishing industry. They're right, of course, but I'm pissed because they don't have enough copies of my books; they're already sold out.

I start out my lecture by recalling that I visited this store a long time ago, when I was first producing *On Our Backs* magazine. Most women's bookstores, like this one, wouldn't carry OOB, they were so offended by its sexual nature.

"Oh, you met me before that," one of the owners calls out from the cash register desk. "At the 'Women in Print' conference, you lit right into me."

Women in Print!—that was a long-deceased coalition of radical feminist bookstores and publishers. They surrounded me at that conference in 1984 like a fucking firing squad, and they told me that my perverted politics would not stand. The biggest publisher in lesbian books crept up to my ear that day and whispered in my ear, "Everyone I know thinks you should be assassinated."

I call back to the bookstore owner. "What did I say to you? I'm sorry, I don't even remember." I didn't recall her at all, I can only hear that little whisper.

The woman turned crimson. Again, I seemed to be making someone confess who hadn't planned on talking at all. "You said I should see a shrink; you said that if I hated sex so much, I should see someone about it."

The floor of two hundred hippie college girls sitting between us fell quiet. If I didn't say something right away, this woman was going to crumble like a piece of dough. "Oh, that sounds so cruel; that's so awful I spoke to you that way," I said. "I hate that, when people pass judgments on you that ring in your ears long after they've forgotten them entirely."

"But it didn't help," she said.

Portland, Oregon

I arrive for my first hotel stay, instead of crashing with friends. I don't know anyone in town, but this is my very favorite hotel, The Heathman. It's old-Portland luxury, and I feel like the mistress of a lumber baron. Powell's, the bookstore that's sponsoring me, is one of the largest in the world. They have acres of books and a big auditorium to host my event.

Mommy's Little Girl

Backstage at the theater, while I waited in the wings, I was surrounded by props and stagecraft for a children's production of *Dracula*. An activist hooker introduced me onstage, laying on a thick cream of all my credentials and credits. I made my entrance by snatching one of the black crosses on the floor and carrying it above my head.

After my show, two beautiful women came up to my side and lightly pressed my shoulders. "We know you must be exhausted," says one. And then the other, "We want you to call us anytime tonight if we can take care of you. We're professionals." They didn't blush at all; they winked.

I was dead tired and had to drive into Seattle by nine a.m., but when I got back to my lumber-baron suite, I called them. You can't turn away such gifts. They made love to me, and massaged me, and tucked me in.

Seattle

I still shimmer the next day from my two angels' ministrations. I don't remember their names, only their plush wings, glossy hair, and magic hands. It's easy to float into Bailey Coy Bookstore, in the gay center of town. A leader of the Washington Bar Association comes up to congratulate me for something.

I sign a few breasts, hands, some books; and my best friend in Seattle brings her parents up to meet me. They are flushed, the father more than the mom. "I'm sorry we have to leave so soon," her mother says, as graceful as her daughter. I wonder if I have any marks on my neck.

The next day I got to be on the radio with Kennedy, a notorious former MTV VJ who was the only one I ever liked because she was a smart aleck who wore thick glasses. She's also a little potty-mouth, who militantly kept her virginity until she got officially engaged a year ago. Kennedy was once notorious for her romantic obsession with Dan Quayle, and I tell her I had a rather erotic relationship with him myself.

"Oh, my fantasies were never sexual," she says. "It was more like me saying, 'Danny, honey, do want some soy milk in your coffee?' and then he'd say, 'Oh no, sweetheart, just honey.'"

Detroit

It's just as ugly as I remember it, from when I was last here in 1977. I was an community organizer here, which is commie-speak for getting in a whole lot of trouble. During my last week in Detroit I was declared a "menace to society" in Superior Court.

Nowadays, only two auto plants in town are still open, compared to the dozen where I used to leaflet. The original Henry Ford factory is windowless—growing weeds and filling up with dog shit.

I go visit my old comrade, Jane, and convince her that we should go look at the house we shared together when we were both young rads. At the time, she was twenty-seven, and I was her brand new seventeen-year-old roommate. I was a considerate, if immature, roommate, but I accidentally got us evicted one night for throwing an "interracial dinner party"—if you could call it that. I can't stand to think how the landlord described it when he called the cops on us. Probably something like, "fucking niggers in that white girl's apartment."

But that night, there was no fucking going on. I was cooking spaghetti for a bunch of other teenagers, after a high school antiapartheid conference we'd hosted downtown. Jane was at work at the Fleetwood plant, where she was a steward. The pasta was just about to boil when six cops showed up at the door. It's weird how you remember something so slight in the moment before something awful happens.

The first one held a gun to my head and pushed me into the living room, pinning my arms behind my back. The others fanned out through the flat. They said they had information that we were harboring a police hostage. I remember the total silence in the house—except for the flushing coming from the toilet.

I looked at little Yolanda sitting terrified on the sofa, and I cursed myself, because we'd told her mother she was attending a YWCA conference.

I don't know why the Magnificent Six pulled back after that entrance, but they did. They told me I was evicted and had twenty-four hours to get out. "But you're not the landlord!" I said, and they looked at me in disbelief. "Twenty-four hours," said the fat one, who had put me in die half nelson.

We were so pathetically innocent—no one had lit up a joint yet, or was necking with their top up over their head. We did do all that stuff, but we weren't doing it at that moment—everyone was starving waiting on my spaghetti.

Twenty years later, I was ready to visit the ghosts.

"C'mon, let's go to Highland Park," I said to Jane, and she agreed.

"It's called an *Empowerment Area* now," she said, making me laugh.

"That sounds like you get a vibrator if you move in."

It was pouring rain when we drove up Woodward Avenue Our neighborhood, Pasadena Street, is completely uninhabited except for one house, which has gardenias growing inside burglar-bar flower boxes. Every other house is empty. Every other window of every single house is shattered. There are no doors on any of the standing buildings. In our old yard, at Number 73, there's a Mylar balloon limping from a suing on the sycamore tree.

A clap of thunder rumbled loose, and the sky turned so dark that it looked more like midnight than noon. "C'mon, let's check it out before it starts pouring!" I yelled, dragging Jane across the puddles and up what was left of the porch stairs.

"Hey, what happened to those hillbillies who lived here? Did they think the white tide was going to roll in and save them, or what?"

The old lady upstairs was too scared to go out," Jane said. "I'd go get her milk for her, 'cause she was just petrified. She must be dead by now."

I stepped into the center of our old living room, now a bird's nest of smashed fixtures, smashed plaster, and smashed everything else. This building didn't naturally decompose; it had been destroyed by man. The copper wire had been pulled out of the walls, everything had been yanked and broken. The rain fell inside, pooling everywhere, but the water was the most graceful of all the elements that had transformed this place.

"That old lady was tripping," I said. "This was the most mellow place I ever lived as a white person in America."

It's true, no one was ever threatened by my presence in Detroit, or thought I had anything to prove. People must have thought I was a white girl married into a black family; and in a way, they were right. I didn't realize what a heavy load white folks' prejudice was to carry around until I lived without it. If you lived in Detroit when the recession set in, people figured you belonged and left it at that.

Jane whimpered in the living room, unable to take another step into the abyss. "What if there are rats?"

I had on boots, and I kept storming through the rubble into the back of the apartment to see if my old bedroom was still standing. Jane answered her own question: "I guess there are no rats—there's no food here."

That night I spoke at Wayne State. I was introduced by the magenta-haired female president of the Student Union, who Jane told me was a CP member.

"I didn't know anyone under eighty was in the Communist Party!" I said. "And I don't think they let you dye your hair, either...."

Jane told me they'd changed, just like we had.

"But this chick is planning a sex party for next week, and she told me she's really bummed that I'm going to miss it!" I wasn't ready to let go. "CP members don't throw sex parties!"

Minneapolis

I felt like kissing my author escort, Markie. He carried all my bags and helped me into a warm four-wheel-drive vehicle with hot cocoa in the drink caddie

I was due to speak in a Catholic university chapel the first night, with a couple of interviews beforehand, but I asked Markie if he was up for doing something different before we began the grind.

"I want to go find my grandmother's grave," I told him. "She's buried in a cemetery in St. Paul, in what used to be the Irish neighborhood, but it's now black. My mom gave me a map that's like, 'Forty steps right, one step left,' like a pirate treasure map."

Markie was already racing toward the cemetery; he knew just where it was, because he grew up here too. I could tell he didn't care if I got to the media interview or not which was a good sign. The author's whims come first!

"There was no grave marker before," I continued with the saga, "but I sent her some money last year to order one I told her, 'Mom, you and Chick {that's her last sister)) are never going to agree on this gravestone. And then you'll die and she still won't have one—well, that was kind of harsh to say because I knew it would make her cry. But talk about crying—my grandmother died in 1938, and nobody's agreed on anything or done anything since!"

Markie nodded sympathetically, and since he is Irish Catholic, I knew he understood perfectly. "It was only seven hundred dollars," I said, "which is a lot in one way. But why not just put *something* there and feel more peaceful about it?"

The lady in the cemetery office showed me the record book in which all the bodies are listed. She let me Xerox the pages where the name Agnes Williams O'Halloran is entered, in blue ink, the year before penicillin was released. She died of pneumonia when my mom was twelve. All the record books, new and old, have entries like my grandmother's, handwritten in blue fountain pen. It's so different from the rest of the word-processed world that I felt like stroking the pages, as if they were feathers instead of paper.

We couldn't find her grave. Markie went up one row of twenty, and I went down die next. We kept working our way through the rows—a mile of rows, another mile—without success. The map was like a puzzle, not a guide. I read scores of names on die headstones like lines from a saints notebook-Margaret, Mary, Joseph, Michael, Paul, Theresa, Francis—not a Jennifer or a Jason among them.

Markie called up the cemetery lady on his cell phone, because it was getting dark, and she said, "Oh, I just started working here. I really don't know." I felt like crying and then I looked at Markie and here he was, my knight with a shining cell phone. He looked scared, like he had failed me.

But I said, "You are a total Mensch; don't feel bad. Let's just curse them and be off. I'll be back to St. Paul again, and then I'll tie the grave keepers down until they find my grandmother's stone for me."

The college chapel where I spoke that night was wonderful. The acoustics were beautiful; the altar an elegant stage.

One young woman asked me what I thought about "working with sex workers."

I said, "I don't know what you mean—are you talking about driving them to their jobs?" I was genuinely trying to figure out her euphemism.

"No!" she said, and now it was her turn to change colors. "I mean, I work with them, testing for HIV in a public clinic." I looked harder at her, and I saw she was the twin of that husky man in San Luis Obispo: she wanted to save a whore and marry a stripper, and she didn't know where to begin.

"Your clients want someone who'll love them when they stop working just like the rest of us," I told her.

Markie took me to the airport at one a.m., and kissed me on the mouth.

Boston

I have lots of friends in Boston, so we had a party at Amelia's house. I met Hanne Blank, a woman at the party who's just done a book on fat sex, and she was fat and sexy indeed. She told me that, in her book, she wanted to get right down to people's most crazed fears about fat sex. She said the most freaky fear people had was what would happen to them if a giant fat lady got on top of them to get fucked—would they be smothered?

I hadn't even considered it. But Hanne had consulted with some professional fat dominatrixes, who told her they had made countless porn videos with men who fantasized about getting smothered—dreamed of it, in fart—but such a suffocation wasn't easy to achieve, even on purpose. Another urban legend destroyed.

At dinner we ate Amelia's lasagna that she prepares in endless baking pans, just like the parable of loaves and fishes. I told the table about a 'zine published by my friend Shar, called *Starphkr*, it devoted itself exclusively to people's fantasies with the famous and superfamous. I proposed a toast and a game: "Let's go around the table and everyone has to say what their star-fucking fantasy is."

"A Mulder/Scully sandwich," said Am's boyfriend, picking the stars of the *X Files* TV show. That got things off to a nice start. "Susan Dey!" a film professor offered, which seemed to generate an instant coalition of other men agreeing with him. We contemplated the rest of the Partridge tribe for a while without committing to any others.

"My fantasy is sicker than that," I said. "I would weep from shame but my tummy hurts too much from laughing."

"Oh God, is it Michael Jackson?" the professor asked.

"No, it's Mark Fuhrman, O.J.'s nemesis," I said, and waited for the inevitable screams of disbelief.

I tell them I fantasize about Fuhrman back in my old ghetto apartment in Detroit, being too afraid to go outside and be a white man. When he pulls me to the bed, I unzip his trousers and find his penis, blue-black, almost purple, jutting straight out from his fair torso.

New York

Tina Turner was in my hotel elevator. I got into the lift, and there was a woman singing to herself—you know, the way you do when you don't even know that you're humming. I was so charmed, I started to say, "It's so nice to hear someone singing in the elevator"—but I didn't even get past the "It's—" because she woke out of her reverie and noticed I was there, ducking her chin down to her chest.

I looked at that profile—it was Tina! She had tiny feet in loafers with tassels, and a long black cardigan.

Joan Jett came to my reading in a sex-toy store, Toys in Babeland. In LA, I would have snarled at such celebrity sightings, but in New York I was euphoric I don't know Joan Jett's profile at all, just her rebel yell. I was just signing autographs when a woman in line with spiky hair and wicked tattoos asked me to dedicate some books she brought from home "To Joan." I liked the collection she brought; they were my favorites. She turned to leave and the two girls standing in line behind her rushed into my arms with gushing squeals: "That was JOAN JETT! Ohmigod, she asked you to write her name, 'Joan,' like she was nobody!" (Well, what else was she going to say, "Nancy"?)

There are more stars in LA than NYC; but they aren't singing in the elevator, and they don't come to my readings with their erotica clasped to their breast.

The storekeeper ran down the street to catch the rock star, and implored her to come back for a picture. Now that I knew who she was, I was embarrassed, and so was Joan. I'm sure we both looked bright red in the flash of the camera.

In New York, audiences seemed to have a meter running. I felt as if their time were money, and I wanted to quote a Greg Brown lyric to them: Time ain't money when all you got is time." For the first time on my tour the bookstore crowds were quiet—stone quiet.

"What's the matter?" I asked one night.

"No one here is having sex," someone snorted from the back.

You all look at me like I'm the only one who ever has, I thought to myself. They were like the characters in Jerry Stahl's porn film *Café Flesh,* who can't have sex anymore, so they put the freaks who still can do it into a cabaret show and make them perform the act.

The second day I went to visit my friend Joe who works in Christie's auction house. They have a huge antique book inventory, including Bibles that have the page edges secretly, and pornographically, embossed. When you shut the book tight, and look at the edges of the book, the gold leaf reveals itself to be an obscene tableau of debauchery. Joe showed me several Gutenberg specials like this, and then we went down the street to eat kashka varnikes and brisket. That was so good, it was like having sex in New York City at last. I got overheated and had to lie down before my final appearance at the 92nd Street Y.

"Oh dear," the Y hostess greeted me, "I really don't want to hear what you have to say tonight."

I guess that was a joke, but she looked so unhappy. I wanted to walk gravely onstage, and say, "I cannot talk about sex tonight; I am in New York City and no one wants to know."

Months later, after September 11, I wondered what happened to all those people who didn't want sex, didn't want to talk about it. I predicted a post-attack baby boom of unbelievable proportions. Time ain't money when all you got is each other.

I thought about Paul Krassner in Venice and all the great stories he'd told me about NYC when he was young—about the Village, and the Yippies, and Lenny Bruce, and the great quantities of free love and legal acid. I knew all that grooviness must be here somewhere, but I had to get away from the money people and the grasping people and get back to some little scrap of a song that you could sing in a lift without even trying.

Thanksgiving: Home Again

The good news was that, at the end of my two months on the road, I got on three regional bestseller lists. In book lingo, that means you have a "national" bestseller. A *"New York Times* bestseller" means you are actually national, because it polls a nationwide group of bookstores.

The bad news was that my publisher didn't know my good news: I told them. When I asked if they would reconsider advertising my book, my editor told me that since my advertising budget was cut to nothing in the summer, there was nothing-no amount of books sold or cities visited—that could change it.

Something about her "nothing" made me feel as if that's what all my work had amounted to. If I had stayed home and gone to sleep for a hundred years, it all would have been the same.

Then the publisher's publicist called. She said, her voice a little higher than I'd heard it before, that they'd just had a new round of layoffs. "It's been difficult at first, of course," she said, "but now we believe we have a more effective, tighter, more focused group than ever before!"

"My god," I said. "That's great! If they would only get rid of everyone, then it would be perfect."

The book tour was over, and every author feels like Peggy Lee at this point, dragging on a fag and rasping "Is that all there is?" I met thousands of people, and they touched me— their hands on my body, my pen upon their breasts and books, their thoughts on my mind. It had been a season of touching and blushing. I knew they loved me, but my publisher wouldn't know it if we all fell on top of him at the same time.

My agent told me for the one thousandth time not to take it personally, and I said for the thousandth time that I'm not cut out for this. Now, I had a lot of time and no money, a string bikini with no elastic. A few weeks of hibernation were in order. In the spring maybe, I'd feel my skin begin to color, and then, maybe, I'd write another story.

THE RANDY BELLBOY

TOURING ON THE ROAD has introduced me to a whole new group of erotic friends and teachers. One of my favorites is Adrian Ryan, a bellboy-turned-writer who gave me a first class e-mail tutorial in the practice of creating your own personal hotel scandal.

I first heard from Adrian after I wrote a column about getting lonely and horny on the road, but not always being sure what to do about it. Our e-mail correspondence follows:

Susie Dahl-ink,
    Just read one of your recent *Salon* pieces about your book tour. YOU CRACK MY ASS UP. Before I became a multimedia superstar, I was a graveyard-shift bellman at the Benson Hotel in Portland.
    Let me speak from experience—if it wasn't for road-weary travelers (one or two of them authors!) staying at the hotel, I'd have had no sex life for most of my early twenties. As it was, I saw more action than a Bruce Willis flick. If you get frisky and can't bear to face those terrifyingly sterile hotel sheets solo, call the concierge fer chrissake!
Adrian Ryan

Dear Mr. Ryan,
    Believe me, I've had my eye on the concierge before what exactly do I say when they pick up the phone? I need to know the four-star etiquette!
Susie

Silly!
    You don't call and ask for sex... you call and ask for an IRON or a NEW REMOTE CONTROL or ROOM SERVICE. Then you answer the door in a towel. Voilà! That is, if you can find

a lesbian or heterosexual male hotel employee. That'll be a challenge

xo,

A.

A.,

OK, you're going to need to go gentle and slow with me I have opened the door in my towel, and the staff person has behaved very modesty toward me. Of course they are not about to throw me on the bed, as they could be fired for that. Do I give them eye contact and refuse to look away? Whisper "Open Sesame"? Something Mae West-ish? Please tell me exactly how this has transpired in your experience.

S.

Good heavens! This is quickly becoming "Adrian's Online Correspondence College of the Art and Science of Schtupping the Housekeeping Staff."

As well you know, EVERYONE is a horndog deep down; and there are few, if any, who would turn down a luscious and furtive shag with a willing babe. So the trick lies in the fine, lost art of seduction. Hotel employees are very timid; they will be painfully wary of diving in, dropping their britches, and going to town without firm assurance that there will be no hysterical calls to the front desk should their southward parts be suddenly exposed. They must be coaxed! You need to make the fact that your pants are pounding crystal dear. This requires a bit of bravery and a momentary abandonment of dignity. How bad are you jonesing anyway?

Wait until after eleven **p.m.**, when the graveyard staff comes on shift. They always have time and freedom to play. First go

168

downstairs and check out who's working. The guy or gal parking your car will probably be the one to spirit any late-night requests up to your room, because they will keep a light staff on at night. A little window shopping is a wise play. I mean, you don't want to get all gussied up (or down) to discover Jabba the Hut in a bellman's cap drooling in your doorway with the extra towels you just ordered, do you?

This is also a great time, if the goods are fresh, to make a little flirtatious small talk. You know, "Nice night, when do you get off? Does your cock curve to the left or the right?" —that type of stuff. Discreetly reveal your room number (easy these days, since most hotel keys are coded for security—you can feign a bad memory and have Mr. Bell-Stud decode it for you). When he/she gets the call to your room later, the soil will be tilled, as it were.

When your target arrives at the door, fake trouble with the television or getting the window open. Invite them in to "take a look" at the problem.

We are assuming at this point you are in a towel or other scanty, promising apparel.

Then keep him/her around with idle, mindless chitchat—all the while (this is important!) staring at his/her crotch. A minute or two of polite conversation while your gaze is fixed, basilisk-style, upon their bulging nether regions, and voilà! You're as good as laid!

If at first you don't succeed, call them up again, demanding menial things until they get fed up, and put out for the sake of peace and quiet. Or you can get really bold and just have some of that cheesy hotel porn playing when they arrive Don't be shy!

Mommy's Little Girl

The wage slaves of the better hotels are used to being hit on, and the worst that could happen is they could say no. Or you could wind up with some skinny fairy (like me), braiding each other's hair. What do you have to lose? Go, baby, go!

A.

Dear Addy:

I arrived at the Cambridge Marriott at one **a.m.** last night, with all your instructions in mind. As you recommended, I scanned who was on the skeletal graveyard staff. To my dismay, there was only one old coot who looked like he needed a walker. (Yes, I know, some old coots are fine stuff, but believe me, this one was dose to nodding.) I offered to carry my bags myself, and he gratefully acquiesced.

Upon reaching my room—seventh floor in the back, with two heavy bags in hand—I realized I was too tired for hanky-panky anyway. It was just as well that there were no temptations on the night shift to distract me I flipped on the room's light switch as I considered whether it was necessary to take my clothes off at all, since I was going to fall asleep right away and get a wake-up call at six.

But there was just one little problem.

I picked up the phone and called downstairs. "I need a different room," I said. "There's no bed in here."

"No bed?" Mr. Coot didn't trust his hearing.

"Well, there is an unmade hospital gurney set up here, but I'm not quite ready for that yet. Maybe next week."

I lay down on the shag carpet and waited for my prince to arrive with a new key. I knew it would only take a half hour or so.

So you see, Adrian, I'm ready for action, win or lose, but I need the right furniture, and I need my beauty rest!

Your ever-lovin' fan,

Susie

FARMER IN THE DELL

HE WROTE TO ME, "YOU must be weary," and he was right. His message was one of a hundred e-mails per day that I received on the road: six weeks, twenty-eight stops—the full package book tour.

I invited nearly everyone I met on the road to write to me about their own sexual philosophy. His was a little different.

See, those other ninety-nine messages, they said things like, "I can't get enough of you." It was the sweetest praise I could hear, yet it was that very yearning that exhausted me: there was not enough of me and they always wanted more I was just a girl who couldn't say no, and I couldn't register "empty." By the end of the day, though, I was toast. I didn't want to be Susie Sexpert anymore, I wanted to disappear.

This one man—who addressed my tired bones instead of my diva credentials—read not only my weary mind, but all my exhausted senses. He said he was a farmer. He lived an hour from one of the university hamlets I was visiting. He could drive me out there to the fields where I could watch the new garlic grow. We could walk in the woods, or sit at the lakefront, and do absolutely nothing at all. I salivated as I was reading his offer.

My home is in the central farming community of California. Some of my best friends are farmers, and they feed me well. Writers and farmers share the sentiment that you might as well go broke doing something you love.

I liked this man already, because I appreciate what he does for a living, and because he extended to me the nicest invitation I'd ever received on a book tour: to run away from it all. Still, I had to decline. I had interviews scheduled for nearly every hour that I was in his vicinity; there was no way I could make a polite escape.

A week later, week four out of six, I wrote an article for a national webzine in which I admitted that, despite appearances, it was difficult for a sex goddess to get laid. I confidently spoke for all sex goddesses, since we're such a ratified group. I get lonely on my travels, but I often feel inhibited—and defensive. I don't want to be someone's prize—or, worse, a disappointment. I don't want to perform.

The farmer read my article, and he wrote me again. This time, he said that, truth be told, he did fantasize about making love to me—but that his doubts were as real as mine. He liked that I promised fans to be "bad in bed." He said it was a relief.

I couldn't dismiss him as easily as I had the other e-mails, like the one that said: "I am a forty-three-year-old attorney in Las Vegas who is well-endowed. Call me when you arrive."

No, the farmer wrote well, and that always touches me. He was lyrical about his environment, and his kindness was a genuine aphrodisiac. Still, I was wary—this could all be a ruse, an Internet pose job. I wrote the farmer back:

"Things are always so different face-to-face. I hope, when I speak in the city, that you'll come and introduce yourself to me."

I was at a university lecturer's hall, signing books at the back of an auditorium. He came up to me at the very end: the end of a glorious night, a crowd of five hundred readers, and about the same number of autographs on both breasts and books. While on my ninth glass of iced tea, he walked up to the table. In my mania, I'd forgotten entirely about my invitation. What I saw was a six-foot-tall man with graying, curly, long hair, waiting at the end of the line. He was so shy that, despite his height and looks, he didn't stand out in the crowd. He put out his hand and said, "Hello, I'm the farmer."

For a second, my mind recognized nothing; he sounded like a recording from a child's pull toy. I almost replied, "Hello, I'm the author!"

Then my mind's eye uncrossed, and I leapt from behind the table to greet him. He was real, and I gave him a great hug. He embraced me back, and though I remembered he'd said his hands were rough, they weren't harsh at all. I liked his hands right away.

That night I went back to my antiseptic hotel room, put the starched pillow over my head, and started to fantasize about the farmer: his body over me fucking me his hands on my breasts. I pulled myself out of my reverie long enough to grab my laptop and find his address:

Dear Farmer:

I liked meeting you so much tonight. Now I can't get you, or your invitation, off my mind. If I cancel some of my media junk tomorrow, I can get away for four hours—is that ridiculous?

I went to sleep happily—knowing that, if nothing else, I would have him in my dreams. In the morning, I checked my messages:

Susie,

We are planting this morning, but yes, I can finish by the afternoon and come pick you up. It's a beautiful day for you to come out here.

It was a beautiful day. My travels in the Northeast have always been urban, and I had never seen the fall colors of the countryside.

He came for me in his red pickup; and it might as well have been a pumpkin coach, for I felt as if I was going to the most magnificent ball—I was leaving Susie Bright, Cinder-Writer, far behind me. I would be wordless and childlike for a spell; I would crunch leaves in my hands and get lost in the woods. I could get lost with this garlic grower, in his world that looked like a picture in a snow globe.

There were still people working in the fields when we arrived. It was one o'clock in the afternoon. It's an organic farm, supported largely by customers who buy a share in the harvest. Some of them volunteer on the weekends, or come by to pick up their box of produce. He took me to his loft, built into a barn, above stacks of acorn squashes, cabbages, and beets. His personal space was as neat as a ship's cabin. The sun was still high, and it poured into the skylights over his bed and desk. I couldn't help but stare at that bed, so different from my hotel accommodations. It was a plump cloud of down comforters and pillows, high off the floor. I wanted to dive into it and never come up. I searched his walls for a clock: I had three and a half hours left.

"Can we just lie down and pretend that we've known each other for years?" I demonstrated by kicking off my boots and letting myself fall backward onto the cloud, arms akimbo. He followed me, and I circled my leg over his waist, as if we went to bed together this way every night.

"Is it too much?" I said. "I know this is a little crazy, but I like you, and I like to pretend..." Chest to chest, I stopped the chatter; I felt my heart pounding then his. Easy to touch him, easy to talk, but it was hard to look into each other's eyes this close.

Why did anyone ever come up with the term "casual sex"? There's nothing casual about it, no matter how brief it is, unless you can avert your eyes entirely. We did take that look, we did it—and there was all the fear and desire waiting for us. As rare as it was for me to steal four hours with a stranger, it was obviously something entirely untried by him. He was no Las Vegas attorney.

I was the one pushing everything forward now, first my assault on his cloud bed, then peeling off my shirt and tugging at his belt. Was I going too fast for him? I know it's the opposite of the dating advice that every young woman receives. But in my experience, it's men who apply the brakes, who wear their hearts on their sleeves, barely protected by a thin pocket of doubt.

We started to make out in earnest. His hand teased my cunt, and I began to happily lose my mind. I was also going to lose my bladder in a minute if I didn't get up. "Where's your bathroom?" I asked, kissing him to hold my place as I swam out of the featherbed.

In the bathroom, I searched for the toilet paper roll and saw his reading matter: the *Farmers' Almanac,* of course, then *Calvin and Hobbes, Harper's,* and yes, there, an old copy of the book I wrote the year after my daughter was born.

I looked so slim and glamorous in that old book-cover photo: my hair dark as oil, my cleavage squeezed tight in a latex dress. I glanced down from the book cover to my lap—the particular view I had on the toilet—and I could see several gray hairs on my mons, right below my round belly.

Christ, get that Book Cover Chick outta here! What a frightening comparison. I'm not going to let her awesome image prey upon my mind and wilt away my hard clit.

I came out of the bathroom naked, a little self-conscious now, looking straight across the long room at my farmer in bed. For the first time I saw that he had a satin hat box under his nightstand, and he was opening it. He said something about a condom that he held between his fingers, but my attention was drawn by what else was in the box.

There was *my* vibrator, and next to it, *my* lube, I name these items possessively, because this particular vibrator is the kind I promoted for years, and his water-soluble lubricant is the one I've told millions was the most slippery and wouldn't kill your taste buds with the flavor of nonoxynol-9.

I wasn't an official spokesperson for these toys; I was just their most public user who wrote about such things prolifically, back in the days when such products had no promotion of their own. It had a remarkable effect. There's not a town I've visited where some woman doesn't say to me, "You sold me my first vibrator; I owe you my first orgasm."

Okay, I believed them, but I never met my efforts head-on like this in my own sex life Sure I've had lovers with chests of sex toys, but they were part of the in-crowd; we shared and collected these things like baseball cards. When I actually had sex with civilians, outside the sex world, they didn't have any of this stuff. They brought their bodies and maybe some good wine and that was it!

I glanced back at the condom in his hand—yes, that was one of "my" brands, too. I had a vision of Susie Cover Girl in her latex dress, lying on the other side of the farmer, smiling. She'd been here before me!

Was she smirking, or just letting me know that my good works had come before me? I didn't know whether I wanted to push her off the bed, or shake her shoulders and demand, "Where does it end?"

I must have shoved my new lover as my mind played out this pantomime, because he stopped my train of thought: "What's going on? Where are you, Susie?"

I sighed and reached into the box to raise the Hitachi up to eye level. "It's great you have this here; I feel right at home I'm just surprised."

He said something about his last girlfriend, it being her favorite as well—how she was in the audience the night before at my lecture and how it had been a bittersweet reunion. "Your books were one of the things we shared together, but then I haven't seen her since I broke it off a few months ago. It was good to see her again, with you in the room, actually. She has a new boyfriend now; she introduced him to me."

I imagined this girl, and her new man, in another bedroom together, with some of the same accessories. I felt like I had tiptoed into a million bedrooms without realizing it, an inveterate sleepwalker.

The farmer rested his weight upon me and pressed his palms—not rough, just right—on the hollows of my shut eyelids. I felt myself sink deeper into the cloud, in absolute darkness, the pressure of his hands blotting out every other thought except my ache, and his cock inside my pussy. I felt close to tears, and that was a relief sweeter than orgasm. Offstage at last, sweet and bottomless. I'll never write another book again.

We woke up from the sex and the nap. I looked up at the dock. I had one more hour. There was late afternoon October sun, hot like summer, but disappearing twice as fast. "Let me show you around the farm before it gets any darker," he said. "Yeah, I want to see garlic grow in real time," I said. We climbed out of the loft, still sticky in our clothes, and I ran right down the dirt path into the green stalks, leaving everything else behind me.

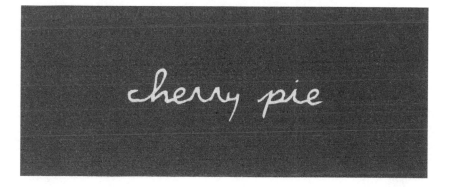

ETERNAL CHERRY DEVOTION PIE

SOMETIMES YOU NEED TO PREPARE a meal that will make someone fall in love with you. Sometimes you need a dessert with an enchantment so strong that your lover will never leave you, no matter what the temptation.

When you're ready for such a strong potion, you need to make Eternal Cherry Devotion Pie.

Don't make this pie if you're just toying with someone—you'll be sorry. Don't make this pie for your lover if you don't want him or her by your side forever, only to moan at your grave when you're gone. This is serious stuff.

If you make it for children, it will simply make their cheeks glow and put a spring in their step; so that's one way to play it safe. They'll always be Mommy's Little Girls.

Fresh cherry pie tastes absolutely nothing like pie with canned cherry filling—it has no more in common with such an ingredient than it does with laundry detergent.

Cherries are only truly in season during the first few weeks of summer, so this pie must be prepared in June if it's to have its intended effect.

Directions

Get 3 lbs. of cherries, half of them the dark red Bing, and half of them yellow Queen Anne (sometimes called Rainier).

Pit the cherries, and then let them soak in a mixture of 3 T. tapioca, half a teacup of sugar, a splash of brandy, a pinch of cinnamon and allspice, 2 tsp. of lemon juice, 1 tsp. of lemon zest, and a drop of almond extract.

While the flavors of the cherry mixture are infusing, make your pie crust:

Fill a glass with ice and a little water and let it sit for later. Put 2-1/2 c high protein white flour, 2 T. sugar, and 1 tsp. salt in food processor. Pulse to mix them.

Chip twelve tablespoons of unsalted cold butter into the food processor, and give it a handful of one-second pulses. The butter will be cut into the flour in odd lumps and pea-size bits.

The mixture should be irregular; that's what makes it flakey.

Add blobs of Crisco (8 T.) and do another five pulses or so. Put dough into large bowl.

Go get your glass of now-perfect ice water. Sprinkle 6 T. of the ice water into the dry mixture, just a little at a time, and mix each splash in with a rubber or wooden spatula. Keep sprinkling and mixing several drops at a time, turning the bowl.

The point is not to just dump the water in one place and then try to work it in; it won't be even, and you'll end up adding too much water.

Now your dough is ready to roll.

Pat it into two even-sized balls; press each into a saucer-size disk. Wrap them in separate pieces of wax paper and put them in the fridge for at least a half hour. Go write an erotic poem and the time will fly right by.

Rolling for Virgins:

Unfold one of the chilled dough disks onto a breadboard-sized piece of wax paper. (Leave second disk chilling in fridge.)

Now put another piece of wax paper the same size on top of the dough. The disk is sandwiched in between the two pieces of wax paper. Your rolling pin will never touch the dough while you're rolling it out.

Take a rolling pin and roll a few decisive strokes from the center in each direction, like a clock hand. After a few strokes, lift the wax paper off the dough and turn the dough upside down onto the other sheet of wax paper.

Keep doing this until the dough is as big as you like. You won't need to add extra flour.

Remember the dough is thickest in the middle, so always roll from the middle out. Make it roughly a circle, about an inch or so bigger than your pie pan. Remove the top sheet of wax paper.

Take the bottom wax paper that has the dough on it and lay it upside down over your pie pan. Peel the paper off the back, and settle the pie dough into the pan.

Pour your cherry mélange into the pie shell and put in the refrigerator.

Take out the other disk of dough—you're going to make the top lattice crust now. Roll out just as you did for the bottom crust.

When you have your 12-inch circle, take a knife and cut the dough vertically into half-inch strips.

Mommy's Little Girl

Here's the big secret about lattice crusts: yes, you can be crafty and do it so that it is a perfect basket weave. But *who cares.* It looks totally adorable no matter how you lay the strips down, and it's actually more personal just to make it up yourself.

Meditate on your beloved, and lay down the strips any way you choose so that the topping is basically covered, with little peek-a-boo holes between the strips. Flute the edges with your fingertips, pressing them like a tender lover.

Bake at 400 degrees for 20 minutes. Turn down heat to 350 degrees and bake another 30 minutes. Cool pie on rack for an hour. Prepare for divination and devotion.

CREDITS

Earlier and different versions of "My Mommy's Job" "First-Grade Values," "Checkmate," "How to Ruin Any Woman's Sex Life in Thirty Days or Less," "Checking Out," "The Real Man's Guide to Lousy Sex," "Intern Phobia," "Old and in the Nude," "Still Insatiable," "Dirty Bookstore Docent," "How Much Wood?," and "The Randy Bellboy" first appeared in Salon.com in "Susie Bright's Sexpert Opinion" column.

Earlier versions of "The Birthing Day Party" and "Boys Who Want Burgers" first appeared in Libida.com. An earlier and different version of "The Buzz of the Century" first appeared in *Playboy*. "Pornographic Futures" first appeared in *Yahoo Internet Life*. "Book Tour Diary" first appeared in *The Realist*.

Thanks to Spain Rodriguez for the cherry pie illustration and Aretha Bright for the picture of Sally Binford. Thank you to Stephen Goddard and Maria Elena Buszek at Kansas University for their inspiration and direction of the Vargas Pinups exhibition.

WHO IS SUSIE BRIGHT?

You can find all of Susie Bright's books, audio, and movies at:
http://astore.amazon.com/susiebrightcom/

In Bed With Susie Bright, weekly audio show:

http://audible.com/susiebright/

Susie Bright's Blog: http://susiebright.com/

SUSIE BRIGHT'S TITLES

Quiver: Gothic and Erotic Short Stories, editor

X: An Erotic Treasury, editor

The Best American Erotica, 1993-2008, editor

Inspired by Andrea: Essays on Lust, Aggression, Porn, & The Female Gaze

Three Kinds of Asking For It, editor

Three the Hard Way, editor

Mommy's Little Girl: Susie Bright on Sex, Motherhood, Porn, and Cherry Pie

How To Write a Dirty Story

Full Exposure

The Sexual State of the Union

Nothing But the Girl (with Jill Posener)

Herotica, 1, 2, and 3, editor

Sexwise

Susie Bright's Sexual Reality: A Virtual Sex World Reader

Susie Sexpert's Lesbian Sex World